Simple Feasts

Simple Feasts

Appetizers, Main Dishes & Desserts

Marilee Matteson

HOUGHTON MIFFLIN COMPANY · BOSTON

1983

Also by Marilee Matteson
Small Feasts

Copyright © 1983 by Media Projects Incorporated

Library of Congress Cataloging in Publication Data

Main entry under title:

Simple feasts.

Includes index.
1. Cookery (Appetizers)   2. Cookery (Entrées)
3. Desserts.   I. Matteson, Marilee.
TX740.S47   1983   641.8   82-23403
ISBN 0-395-33102-1

Printed in the United States of America

H 10 9 8 7 6 5 4 3 2 1

*Grateful acknowledgment is made to the following individuals and
publishers for their permission to use or reprint the recipes listed
below:*

Arbor House for "Mushroom Soufflé" and "Seafood Fric-
assee" from *The Maurice Moore-Betty Cooking School of Fine
Cooking.* Copyright © 1973 by Maurice Moore-Betty.
Michael C. Batterberry for "Cauliflower with Mustard
Seed Butter," "Lentil Salad," and "Fresh Pickled Mush-
rooms" from *The International Review of Food & Wine.*

(*continued on page vi*)

Acknowledgments

Thanks to the following individuals for valuable assistance at various stages in this endeavor: Gus Francisco and Allen Baillie of Gus Francisco Photography, principal photographers for this volume; Diane Mogelever, home economist, food stylist, and contributor of several recipes; my friend and colleague Elizabeth Esterling, for her recipes and her advice; Rosemarie McMorrow at Dansk International, who graciously provided china, crystal, flatware, linens, and table accessories to enhance our photographs.

Thanks to the following individuals at Media Projects: Carter Smith, its president, for asking me to write this book and for his guidance and advice; Teresa Egan, managing editor, for her help and advice on permissions and other matters; and my editor, Ellen Coffey, with whom I have enjoyed working on *Simple Feasts* and its predecessor, *Small Feasts.*

I also acknowledge the support and cooperation of the following individuals at Houghton Mifflin: my editor, Linda Glick, copy editors Luise Erdmann and Sarah Flynn, and designers Louise Noble and Cope Cumpston.

M.M.

Contents

Introduction

SIMPLE FEASTS is three cookbooks: Appetizers, Main Dishes, and Desserts. The three elements go together naturally. With today's trend toward lighter meals, one dish from each section will provide an ample repast for your family or for guests — the menus on pages xii–xiv suggest a number of appealing combinations. Add one of your favorite salads, a complementary vegetable dish, and perhaps a wholesome bread, for a substantial, hearty meal. You can also refer to each section of SIMPLE FEASTS as a cookbook that stands on its own.

The well-stocked larder for SIMPLE FEASTS assures that staples and useful extra ingredients for quick and easy meals are always on hand. Follow these guidelines and add favorites of your own; you will always be prepared for good eating and gracious entertaining as the whim or the need overtakes you.

The list that follows suggests items to keep on hand whenever possible — staples and spices, vegetables and fresh herbs most often used in cooking, frozen foods, and wines. Many meat and poultry dishes can be made with leftovers from other meals; freeze the leftovers until you are ready to use them.

Pantry:

anchovies	Worcestershire sauce
minced clams	bouillon
sardines	chicken broth
canned tunafish	consommé
liver pâté	vichyssoise
small canned ham	canned soups
deviled ham	dried onion soup mix
artichoke hearts	herb stuffing mix
sliced beets	clam juice
whole kernel corn	tomato juice
olives	pastas
hearts of palm	rice
pimiento	rice mixes
Tabasco sauce	wild rice
tomatoes	biscuit mix
tomato paste	dry milk
tomato sauce	

Herbs and spices:

arrowroot	dry mustard
basil	paprika
bay leaves	black pepper
cinnamon	white pepper
curry	rosemary
dill	thyme
marjoram	

Note: Your kitchen should really have two pepper mills: one for black pepper, one for white. Freshly ground pepper tastes much better; white pepper should always be used in a light-colored soup, sauce, soufflé, or other dish.

Vegetables:
garlic	potatoes
onions	shallots

Oils:
corn oil *or* vegetable oil	olive oil

Vinegars:
cider vinegar	tarragon vinegar
red wine vinegar	

Refrigerator:
Cheddar cheese	parsley
cream cheese	capers
Gruyère cheese	horseradish
Parmesan cheese	barbecue sauce
bacon	chili sauce
carrots	ketchup
boiled ham	mayonnaise
lemons	mustards

Freezer:
chicken and leftover cooked chicken	frozen shrimp, raw or cooked
crabmeat	leftover roast meats

Wines:
Madeira	white wine
dry sherry	red wine
vermouth	

Note: Leftover wine should be transferred to a small bottle just big enough to hold it, so air cannot spoil the flavor.

SIMPLE FEASTS contains over three hundred and fifty recipes in all, including recipes from many names well known in the world of fine food. These contributors include:

Jean Anderson, author of ten cookbooks, including *Jean Anderson's Processor Cooking* and the comprehensive *Jean Anderson Cooks.*

Barbetta's Restaurant in New York City, this year celebrating seventy-five years of serving fine Italian cuisine in a charming Old World atmosphere.

Michael Batterberry, respected cook and wine connoisseur, the founder and former editor in chief of *The International Review of Food & Wine.*

Jean Charles Berruet, a native of Normandy and the owner-chef of the Chanticleer restaurant in Siasconset on Nantucket Island.

Ann Cashion, a native Mississippian and a professional cook and pastry chef in San Francisco. Mississippi Mud Cake is her own version of an old southern favorite.

Elizabeth Schneider Colchie, the author of *Ready When You Are,* co-author of *Better Than Store Bought,* and a frequent contributor to food magazines.

Helen Corbitt, a legendary figure of American cuisine, the author of half a dozen cookbooks, and the winner of the highest honors of the food world in America.

George Davis, an artist, chef, and the proprietor of the Morning Glory Café on Nantucket Island.

Elizabeth Esterling, founder of the Paris Cooks school in Washington, D.C., and dessert and bread chef of the Inn at Quogue, Long Island, rated with three stars by the *New York Times*.

Roy F. Gustede, the fifth-generation proprietor-chef of the famous Antoine's restaurant in New Orleans.

Joan Itoh, a weekly columnist for the *Japan Times* and the author of *Rice-Paddy Gourmet* and *Japanese Cooking Now*.

Richard Lavin, who recently put aside a successful career in real estate to realize a lifelong dream and open a restaurant in New York City — Lavin's, featuring American *nouvelle cuisine*.

Maurice Moore-Betty, the author of several cookbooks, a contributor to national food magazines, and the founder of the Maurice Moore-Betty School of Fine Cooking in New York City.

Gloria Pepin, the wife of world-renowned chef and cookbook author Jacques Pepin and a fine cook in her own right.

Wolfgang Puck, former chef and part owner of Ma Maison restaurant, currently owner-chef of Spago restaurant in Los Angeles, and the author of *Modern French Cooking for the American Kitchen*.

Julee Rosso and Sheila Lukins, the founders of the Silver Palate, Manhattan's celebrated gourmet food shop, and the authors of *The Silver Palate Cookbook*.

The Russian Tea Room, famed New York favorite of politicians, musicians, and literary and dramatic lights.

Richard Sax, a chef, caterer, food editor, and the former overseer of the test kitchen at *The International Review of Food & Wine*.

Donald Bruce White, a New York caterer with a long-standing reputation for fine food.

Sallie Y. Williams, a cooking school instructor, lecturer, and the author of *The Art of Presenting Food*.

Helen Witty, the co-author with Elizabeth Schneider Colchie of *Better Than Store Bought* and a frequent contributor to food magazines.

Note: A simple referral system cross-references recipes for use with one another. A recipe with capitals — for example, Quick Basic Pie Crust — that appears in an introduction, ingredient list, note, or variation can be found in the index and easily located in the text.

Menus

The Boss Is Coming to Dinner
Eggs Cresson
Casserole-roasted Veal
Chocolate Cheesecake

An Elegant Luncheon
Quick Quiche
Cold Pasta & Seafood Salad
Poached Pears

From the Sea
Cold Fish Mousse
Scallops Marinara
Apple Brandy Apples

A Touch of the East
Rumaki
Joan Itoh's Boiled Shrimps
    & Cauliflower
Oriental Oranges

A Winter's Night
Scallop Soup
Roast Lamb with Mustard & Ginger
Brown Betty

Elegant Simplicity
Shrimp Bisque
Maurice Moore-Betty's Turkey Scalloppine
    with Marsala
Angel Pie

A Summer's Eve
Ceviche
Sallie Y. Williams's Summer Spaghetti
Strawberries in Champagne

An Italian Supper
Antipasto Salad
Lynn's Lasagna
Richard Sax's Stuffed Italian Peaches

A Touch of Greece
Mushrooms à la Grecque
Moussaka
Honey Apples

Dinner & Bridge
Stuffed Mushrooms
Broiled Orange Chicken
Easy Coffee Mousse

After an Autumn Walk
Cocktail Hot Dogs
Mixed Grill
Brandied Fruit Compote

No-Time-to-Cook Buffet
Cheese Straws
Lazy Beef Stew
Ten-Minute Chocolate Pie

A Candlelight Dinner
Artichokes Ravigote
Veal Scallops with Orange
Creamy Zabaglione

A French Bistro Dinner
Crudité Plate
Choucroute Garnie
Crème Caramel

Delightfully Informal
Marinated Broccoli
Jean Anderson's Mushroom & Shallot
   Stuffed Hamburgers
Pecan Crunch Pie

A Vegetarian Feast
Guacamole
Linguine Primavera
Barbetta Restaurant's Pears Baked in Wine

Fun & Fancy
Smoked Salmon Soufflé
Veal Rolls with Tomato Sauce
Tipsy Raspberries

Backyard Barbecue
Basic Deviled Eggs
Souvlakia
No-Bake Brownies

Light & Lovely
Morning Glory Café Chicken Soup
Stir-fried Shrimp & Vegetables
Ambrosia

Everybody's Favorite
Molded Pâté
Fillet of Sole with Mushrooms
Apple-Blueberry Crisp

So Chic
Stuffed Eggs Mornay
Elizabeth Esterling's Veal Scallops with
   Artichokes
Key Lime Pie

Scrumptious
Antoine's Oysters Thermidor
Ragout of Veal & Eggplant
Strawberry Tart

Super Brunch
Baked Eggplant with Sherry
Scrambled Eggs with Smoked Salmon
Chilled Apple Cream

The Crowd's Coming
Zucchini Squares
Chili con Carne
Carrot Cake from the Morning Glory Café

After the Cocktail Party
Helen Witty's Chicken Livers in Madeira
Turkey Tetrazzini
Danish Apple Cake

A Special Occasion
Wolfgang Puck's Smoked Fish Mousse
Honeyed Chicken
Cantaloupe Cocktail

Before the Concert
Avocado Mold
Coq au Vin
Peach Melba

Fish Lover's Paradise
Bacon-wrapped Scallops
Broiled Swordfish with Béarnaise Sauce
Ginger Mousse

Après-Ski
Liptauer Cheese Spread
Chicken Kebabs
Speedy Lemon Pie

Hearty Fare
Anchovies & Roasted Red Peppers
Ragout of Lamb
Cream Cheese Pie

Dinner for Susie's Teacher
Marinated Shrimp
Chicken Cutlets in Cream
Orange Freezer Pie

Let's Dress Up
Boursin-style Cheese
Fillet of Sole Florentine
Caramelized Pears

The Men Are Cooking
Crabmeat Crackers
Grilled Butterflied Lamb
Bananas Flambées

Can't Beat This One
Marinated Mushrooms
Chinese Spareribs
Grand Marnier Mousse

Afterward We'll Go to a Disco
Fancy Tomatoes
Hungarian Goulash
Chilled Strawberry Soufflé

Appetizers

Appetizers

SIMPLE FEASTS *begins with Appetizers — enough for cocktail parties and first courses for all seasons. Here are recipes from the sublimely simple to the highly sophisticated, but no recipe is difficult, and most take little time in the kitchen. Many can be prepared well ahead of time.*

Cheese Bites, with Cheddar cheese and bacon, can be made ahead and frozen in plastic bags. They can be thawed and baked in minutes if company comes unannounced. Liptauer Cheese Spread can be served on rounds of dark bread or stuffed into vegetable containers. Cheese Logs are perennial party favorites and a wonderful way to use up leftover cheese. Cheese Straws, Cheese Crackers, and Cheese Cookies are all variations on a popular theme. Parmesan Puffs and Roquefort Puffs are just a little more adventurous.

Fish and seafood appetizers are very popular now. Although seafood is expensive, shrimp, for example, is an excellent appetizer investment — a little goes a long way, and the flavor is well worth the price.

Shrimp is a celebrity specialty. Helen Corbitt's Shrimp à la Helen is subtly flavored and quickly broiled. This dish is even better prepared over charcoal. Joan Itoh's Japanese Sweet-&-Sour Little Shrimps can be made with canned or fresh shrimp. If you keep Japanese condiments on hand (they are

sometimes a little hard to track down, but the search will take you to interesting places), these and other dishes are easily made. Donald Bruce White's Marinated Shrimp with Fresh Snow Peas is an American rendition of an Oriental idea. Another version of Marinated Shrimp "cooks" itself overnight. Take your pick.

Bacon-wrapped Scallops provide an excellent contrast of texture and flavor — and happily, 1 pound of sea scallops makes 60 bite-sized portions. Tapenade (anchovy-tuna dip), easily made in a food processor or blender, is also very versatile. Serve it as a dip for raw vegetables or as a first course, spooned over halves of hard-cooked egg.

Appetizers made with meat or poultry are traditional party fare. Tiny meatballs are always a favorite, so we have provided several versions, including Helen Corbitt's, made with Smithfield ham spread and Roquefort cheese added to the ground beef. There are several versions of cocktail frankfurters, too — with a delicious mustard-currant sauce; atop a cabbage centerpiece accompanied by cheese, shrimp, and salami; heated in a sauce flavored with sherry and brown sugar and served in a chafing dish. Tried and true hors d'oeuvres are here — Hot Beef Dip, Salami "Pies," Ribbon Sandwiches of deviled ham and egg — as well as the elegant and unusual — Don-

ald Bruce White's *Skewered Smoked Turkey & Watermelon Rind* and his impressive but easy *Fresh Figs with Prosciutto*.

Vegetable appetizers are especially welcome in the summer, and a plate of appetizers makes a lovely light summer meal. Try cherry tomatoes filled with tuna salad, *Marinated Broccoli*, and *Marinated Mushrooms*. Fill *Cucumber Cups with Salmon Pâté*. When the weather turns cold, vegetables are still appropriate. Serve hot mushrooms stuffed with sausage or bread crumbs. Try a *Hot Onion Dip*, crisp golden slices of *Mushroom Rolls*, or flavorful *Spinach Balls* well seasoned with Parmesan cheese.

Raw vegetables are extremely popular, with so many of us conscious of what and how much we eat. Here are dips for crudités — *Curry, Dill,* and a *Lo-Cal* cottage cheese and yogurt combination. The choice of vegetables is up to you.

Soups are traditional first courses, and the selection here is distinctive as well as delicious. Sallie Y. Williams's *Broccoli-Roquefort Soup, Cold Spinach & Basil Soup,* and a *Chicken Soup* from the Morning Glory Café that can be served hot or cold are beginners for highly satisfying meals.

Many appetizers and first courses can easily serve as luncheon dishes or light supper fare. Try Helen Witty's *Chicken Livers in Madeira, Parsleyed Ham (Jambon Persillé), Stuffed Eggs Mornay,* or the Silver Palate's rich *Tortellini in Gorgonzola Cream.* Wolfgang Puck's *Smoked Fish Mousse,* our *Smoked Salmon Soufflé,* and *Ceviche* are all possible luncheon or supper dishes. Vegetable appetizers can also grace a luncheon or supper table — *Toasted Mushroom Sandwiches, Zucchini Squares,* and *Ham & Asparagus Mornay* can all be quite substantial. And soups, too — *She Crab Soup* or *Shrimp Bisque* needs only a salad and bread (and perhaps dessert) to make a successful meal.

Eggs & Cheese

Basic Deviled Eggs
Deviled Eggs in Aspic
The Russian Tea Room's Russian
  Egg Salad
Eggs Cresson
Stuffed Eggs Mornay
Quick Quiche
The Silver Palate's Tortellini with
  Gorgonzola Cream Sauce
Filled Edam Cheese
Double Cheese Canapés

Liptauer Cheese Spread
Boursin-style Cheese
Cheese Log
Olive-Cheese Balls
Cheese Bites
Cheese Straws
Cheese Cookies
Cheese Crackers
Parmesan Puffs
Souffléed Saltines
Roquefort Puffs

Basic Deviled Eggs

(6 servings)

6 hard-cooked eggs
2 tablespoons Mayonnaise
Celery salt
Freshly ground white pepper
Flavoring (see below)

Cut the eggs in half lengthwise. Remove the yolks and mash them with the remaining ingredients. For a flavoring, use your imagination — mustard, chives, curry powder, chutney, minced bacon, anchovies, minced olives, are all appropriate. Fill the whites with the yolk mixture.

Notes: The yolks can be mashed with flavoring in a food processor.

A pastry bag can be used to fill the egg whites for an attractive presentation.

If there is not enough time to stuff the eggs, mash them and make a spread, flavored as desired.

Deviled Eggs in Aspic

(4–8 servings)

1 recipe Quick Aspic
8 Deviled Eggs
Watercress (garnish)
Watercress Mayonnaise (garnish)
Olive bits (garnish)
Parsley sprigs (garnish)

Cover the bottom of a ring mold with a thin layer of aspic. Place the mold in the refrigerator or freezer until the aspic is firm. Meanwhile, make the deviled eggs and decorate the tops with bits of olives and parsley or another garnish. Place the eggs in the mold, cut side down, and spoon some of the aspic over them to "glue" them down. Chill again until firm. Spoon in the rest of the aspic and chill to set. Unmold. Garnish with the watercress and watercress mayonnaise before serving.

The Russian Tea Room's Russian Egg Salad

(12 servings)

- 6 hard-cooked eggs
- ½ teaspoon salt
- ¼ teaspoon freshly ground black pepper
- 1 teaspoon dry mustard
- ¼ teaspoon sugar
- 1 teaspoon water
- 1 cup Mayonnaise
- ¼ teaspoon minced garlic
- 1 tablespoon finely minced green onions *or* chives

Cut the eggs into neat, thin rounds. Sprinkle with the salt and pepper. In a bowl place the mustard, sugar, and water and mix to a smooth paste. Add the mayonnaise and garlic. Fold the mixture gently into the eggs with a wooden spoon, taking care not to break the slices. Place in a serving bowl. Top with the green onions or chives. Serve with crackers or toast rounds.

Eggs Cresson

(4 servings)

- 1 bunch watercress, leaves only, minced
- 2 tablespoons minced fresh parsley
- 1 cup Mayonnaise
- 1 tablespoon lemon juice
- 4 hard-cooked eggs

Save a few pretty sprigs of the watercress for a garnish. Combine the first 4 ingredients to make a sauce. If it is too thick, thin it with a little milk. Cut the eggs in half lengthwise and place the cut side down on serving plates. Cover with the sauce and decorate with sprigs of watercress.

Note: The sauce can be made easily in a blender or food processor.

Stuffed Eggs Mornay

(8 servings)

- ½ pound mushrooms, finely chopped
- 6 tablespoons butter
- 4 tablespoons flour
- 2 cups milk
- 8 hard-cooked eggs
- Nutmeg
- Salt and freshly ground black pepper
- 4 slices white toast, with crusts removed
- ½ cup grated Gruyère cheese
- Paprika

In a skillet sauté the mushrooms in 2 tablespoons of the butter. Meanwhile, melt the rest of the butter in a saucepan and mix with the flour. Add the milk and stir to make a cream sauce; season with the nutmeg, salt, and pepper to taste. Halve the eggs lengthwise, remove the yolks, and mash them with the mushrooms. Add some of the cream sauce as a binder. Fill the whites with the mixture.

Preheat the oven to 400°.

Quarter the pieces of toast. Using a flat ovenproof dish just large enough to hold the toast or 8 small baking dishes, place the eggs on the toast quarters. Add the grated cheese to the remaining cream sauce and gently spoon the sauce over the eggs. Sprinkle with the paprika and bake until bubbly, 10 to 15 minutes.

Quick Quiche

(4–6 servings)

- 1½ cups milk
- ½ cup biscuit mix
- 6 tablespoons butter (at room temperature)
- 3 eggs
- Pinch of salt
- 1 cup chopped ham (*or* chicken *or* shrimp *or* other meat or seafood)
- ¾ cup Gruyère *or* Cheddar cheese, grated

Preheat the oven to 350°.

In the bowl of a food processor place the milk, biscuit mix, butter, eggs, and salt and process with the steel blade until well mixed. Pour the batter into an ungreased 9- or 10-inch quiche or pie pan. Sprinkle on the meat and cheese and press down into the batter. Bake for 45 minutes. Let cool for 10 minutes before cutting.

Note: Both the ham and the cheese can be chopped and grated in the processor.

A recipe calling for the use of a food processor can, of course, also be done without one. The chopping and grating can be done by hand; an electric mixer or blender would also produce a smooth batter.

The Silver Palate's Tortellini with Gorgonzola Cream Sauce

(6 servings)

1½ cups dry white vermouth
2¼ cups heavy cream
Freshly ground black pepper
Large pinch of freshly grated nutmeg
2 tablespoons salt
1½ pounds fresh tortellini
¾ pound sweet Gorgonzola cheese, crumbled
1½ tablespoons grated imported Parmesan cheese

In a small heavy saucepan bring the vermouth to a boil and reduce by half. Add the cream, return to a boil, and lower heat to a simmer. Season to taste with the pepper, add the nutmeg, and simmer uncovered for about 15 minutes or until reduced by one third.

Bring 6 quarts of water to a boil in a large pot, add the salt, and cook the tortellini until tender (5 minutes if they are freshly made). Drain and return to the hot pot. Remove the sauce from the heat, stir in half of the Gorgonzola and all the Parmesan, and pour over the tortellini. Set over medium heat and cook gently, stirring constantly, for 5 to 8 minutes, or until the cream has thickened slightly and the tortellini have absorbed some of the sauce.

Divide the tortellini among 6 heated plates, sprinkle each with the reserved Gorgonzola, and serve immediately.

Note: No additional grated cheese is required at the table, but provide your guests with a pepper mill.

Filled Edam Cheese

(12 servings)

1 Edam cheese
½ pound bacon, cooked and crumbled
4 scallions, minced
4 tablespoons parsley, minced
3 ounces cream cheese, softened
Worcestershire sauce to taste

Scoop out the cheese and grate it by hand or in a food processor. Combine it with all the other ingredients and fill the shell of the Edam with the mixture. Serve it with crackers.

Note: Any leftovers can be spread on crackers and baked until bubbly for delicious hot hors d'oeuvres.

Double Cheese Canapés

(20 canapés)

1¼ cups flour
½ teaspoon salt
Pinch of cayenne
¼ cup solid shortening, chilled
3 ounces cream cheese, chilled
1 tablespoon ice water
1 egg yolk, mixed with 1 tablespoon water
1 cup commercial cheese spread, softened
Stuffed olives, sliced

Sift the flour, salt, and cayenne together into a medium-size bowl. Cut the shortening and cream cheese into the flour with a pastry blender or 2 knives until the pieces are the size of small peas. Quickly stir in the water to moisten. Gather the dough together to form a ball. Flatten slightly, wrap in plastic wrap, and chill for ½ hour.

Preheat the oven to 425°.

Roll out the dough to a thickness of ⅛ inch and cut into different shapes with 1½-inch cookie cutters. Place on a cookie sheet, brush with the egg yolk mixture, and bake for 10 minutes or until nicely browned.

Spoon the cheese spread into a pastry bag fitted with a large star tip. Pipe cheese swirls onto each cracker and garnish with an olive slice.

Note: Serve the remaining crackers by themselves in a bowl or basket.

Liptauer Cheese Spread

(12 servings)

12 ounces cream cheese, softened
2 anchovies
1 tablespoon minced onion
1 teaspoon minced capers
½ teaspoon caraway seeds
½ teaspoon paprika
Worcestershire sauce

Combine all the ingredients a few hours before serving to allow the spread to "season." Serve on pumpernickel bread rounds or fill cucumber cups or cherry tomatoes.

Note: This makes a wonderful sandwich with thinly sliced tomatoes on rye or whole-grain bread.

Boursin-style Cheese

(10 servings)

1	clove garlic, cut in half
8	ounces cream cheese, softened
1	tablespoon minced parsley
1	tablespoon minced chives
½	teaspoon dried thyme, crushed
	Freshly ground black pepper
2	tablespoons cream

Rub a mixing bowl with the garlic and discard it. Combine all the other ingredients and refrigerate overnight, covered, so that the flavors will blend. Serve with crackers.

Cheese Log

(15 servings)

6	ounces cream cheese
4	ounces blue cheese
4	ounces grated sharp Cheddar cheese
4	ounces grated Gruyère cheese
2	tablespoons brandy
½	cup chopped walnuts *or* chopped pecans
½	cup chopped parsley

In a bowl combine the first five ingredients. Shape into a long log on waxed paper. On another piece of waxed paper sprinkle the nuts and parsley. Roll the cheese log in this mixture and chill.

Note: This is a wonderful way to use up bits of cheese; use any kind. Cheese logs keep well in the refrigerator — and make nice gifts, too.

Olive-Cheese Balls

(25 balls)

1	cup grated sharp Cheddar cheese
2	tablespoons butter, melted
½	cup flour
⅛	teaspoon dried mustard
	Dash of cayenne pepper
25	large stuffed green olives

Preheat the oven to 400°.

In a bowl gently combine all the ingredients except the olives. Put small pieces of dough in your hand one at a time and roll them around the olives. Bake for 12 to 15 minutes or until golden. Serve hot.

Note: These balls may be frozen; follow the directions given for Cheese Bites.

Cheese Bites

(3 dozen)

½ cup butter
½ cup sharp Cheddar cheese, grated
1 tablespoon Dijon mustard
6 slices crisp bacon, crumbled
1 egg white, stiffly beaten
8–10 pieces thinly sliced bread

Preheat the oven to 400°.

Melt the butter, allow it to cool slightly, and combine it with the cheese, mustard, and bacon. Fold in the egg white. Remove the crusts from the bread and spread the slices with the cheese mixture. Cut into small squares and bake for 10 minutes.

Note: To freeze, place the uncooked squares on a cookie sheet in the freezer. Store the frozen squares in a plastic bag. Bake directly from the freezer for 12 minutes or until golden brown in a 400° oven.

Cheese Straws

(30 pieces)

1 cup flour
½ teaspoon salt
2 tablespoons butter
½ cup freshly grated Gruyère cheese
½ cup freshly grated Parmesan cheese

Preheat the oven to 350°.

In a bowl combine all the ingredients and mix well. Roll out as you would pastry and cut into 3-inch strips. Bake until golden, about 8 to 10 minutes. The straws may be frozen or stored in a tightly covered container.

Note: You can use leftover bits of other cheeses in this recipe.

Cheese Cookies

(24 squares)

½ cup butter
¼ cup grated Swiss *or* Cheddar cheese
1 tablespoon grated Parmesan cheese
½ cup flour
1 egg yolk
Few grains of cayenne pepper
Paprika

Preheat the oven to 350°.

In a bowl cream the butter, then add the cheeses, flour, egg yolk, and cayenne. Roll out the dough into 2 rectangles ⅓ inch thick. Cut the dough into 2-inch squares and place on cookie sheets. Sprinkle with the paprika and bake until the squares are firm and begin to color, about 15 minutes.

Cheese Crackers

(24 crackers)

½ pound Cheddar cheese, grated coarsely
½ cup beer
¼ teaspoon dry mustard
Salt
Cayenne pepper
½ teaspoon cornstarch
2 egg yolks
1 tablespoon cream
24 round crackers

Preheat the oven to 450°.

In the top of a double boiler melt the cheese and add the beer. Make a paste of the mustard by adding a few drops of water and add to the cheese. Season with the salt and a few grains of cayenne to taste and stir until well blended. Make a paste of the cornstarch by adding a few drops of water and add the egg yolks and cream. Combine the egg yolk and cheese mixtures in a saucepan and cook over medium-low heat until smooth and creamy. Spoon the mixture onto the crackers and brown in the oven.

Parmesan Puffs

(24 puffs)

½ cup Parmesan cheese, grated
½ cup minced onion
2 tablespoons minced parsley
½ cup Mayonnaise
Toasted bread rounds
Paprika

Preheat the oven to 400°.

In a bowl combine the first 4 ingredients. Spread on the toast rounds, sprinkle with the paprika, and bake until golden.

Souffléed Saltines

(36 crackers)

36 saltine crackers
Water
¼ pound (1 stick) butter, softened

Soak the crackers in cold water for 20 minutes. Lift them out with a slotted spatula and drain.

Preheat the oven to 400°.

Place the crackers 1½ inches apart on cookie sheets, dot the tops with butter, and bake for ½ hour. *Do not open the oven door.* The crackers may be stored in an airtight container.

Roquefort Puffs

(24 puffs)

4 ounces Roquefort cheese
2 egg whites, stiffly beaten
24 toast rounds
Paprika

Preheat the oven to 400°.

In a bowl cream the cheese, adding a few drops of cream if it is dry. Gently fold in the egg whites. Pile on the toast rounds and bake for 5 minutes. Serve hot.

Fish & Seafood

Cold Fish Mousse
Wolfgang Puck's Smoked Fish Mousse
   (*Mousse de Poisson Fumé*)
Hot Clam Puffs
Clam Dip
Helen Corbitt's Seafood Spread
Crabmeat Crackers
Hot Crab Dip
Antoine's Oysters Thermidor
Jean Anderson's Baked Herring
   Appetizer (*Sill à la Tula Brettman*)
Anchovies & Roasted Red Peppers
Smoked Salmon Soufflé
Salmon Pâté

Egg & Sardine Spread
Cheese-Sardine Ball
Bacon-wrapped Scallops
Ceviche
Wolfgang Puck's Shrimp with Mustard
   (*Crevettes à la Moutarde*)
Helen Corbitt's Shrimp à la Helen
Donald Bruce White's Marinated
   Shrimp with Fresh Snow Peas
Joan Itoh's Sweet-&-Sour Little
   Shrimps
Marinated Shrimp
Tapenade
Helen Corbitt's Pickled Shrimp

Cold Fish Mousse

(8 servings)

1 small onion, sliced
1 cup clam juice
2 sprigs parsley
Salt and freshly ground white pepper
1 envelope unflavored gelatin
2 tablespoons cold water
1 pound fish fillets (sole, flounder, haddock, *or* cod)
1 cup Mayonnaise
1 cup heavy cream

Oil a 6-cup mold and set aside. Place the onion slices in a saucepan with the clam juice, parsley, and a little salt and pepper. Bring to a boil, simmer for 10 minutes, and strain. While the juice is simmering, sprinkle the gelatin onto the cold water in a small saucepan. When the gelatin is soft, add ¼ cup of the strained broth and dissolve completely over low heat. Add to the rest of the broth and mix well.

Place the fish fillets in a skillet and cover with boiling water. Simmer for 10 to 15 minutes, until the fish flakes when tested with a fork. Drain the fillets and place in the bowl of a food processor with the broth and the mayonnaise. Process with the metal blade until very smooth. Transfer the mixture to a large bowl. Whip the cream and fold into the fish. Season to taste. Spoon into the oiled mold and refrigerate for at least 3 hours. Serve on a bed of watercress with Salsa Verde or green mayonnaise.

Wolfgang Puck's Smoked Fish Mousse (Mousse de Poisson Fumé)

(2½ cups)

4 ounces sturgeon, cut in 1-inch pieces
4 ounces smoked salmon, cut in 1-inch pieces
½ teaspoon salt
½ teaspoon freshly ground black pepper
Juice of half a lemon
1 cup heavy cream, whipped
2 ounces red or black caviar

In a food processor, purée the sturgeon. Strain through a *tamis* or fine sieve into a bowl and keep cold. Similarly, purée the smoked salmon. Strain through a *tamis* or fine sieve into a separate bowl and keep cold. Season each fish purée with the salt, pepper, and lemon juice to taste. Fold half the cream into the salmon and half into the sturgeon.

In the bottom of a 3-cup serving dish, spread the sturgeon purée. Sprinkle with half the caviar and top with the salmon purée. Sprinkle the remaining caviar over the top. Chill overnight to give the mousse the desired firm consistency. Do not unmold, but serve from the dish.

Variation: Lox may be substituted for the smoked salmon, in which case omit the salt.

Hot Clam Puffs

(24 puffs)

- 1 7-ounce can minced clams, drained
- 1 egg yolk
- 1 3-ounce package cream cheese, softened
- Few drops Worcestershire sauce
- 1 teaspoon chopped chives
- 1 teaspoon chopped parsley
- 24 toast rounds

Preheat the oven to 350°.

In a bowl combine all the ingredients. Spead on toast rounds and bake until golden brown, about 10 minutes.

Clam Dip

(10 servings)

- 1 8-ounce package cream cheese and chives, softened
- 2 6½-ounce cans minced clams, drained
- Lemon juice
- Worcestershire sauce

In a mixing bowl combine the clams and cheese. Add the lemon juice and Worcestershire to taste. Heat in an ovenproof serving dish until bubbly. (This may also be served cold.)

Helen Corbitt's Seafood Spread

(40–50 canapés)

- 1 cup finely chopped lobster
- 1 cup chopped shrimp
- 1 cup chopped crabmeat
- ¾ cup Russian dressing
- ¼ cup chopped salted pistachio nuts

In a bowl combine the seafood and the Russian dressing. Refrigerate for at least 1 hour. Serve on thin crackers or melba toast, and sprinkle with the chopped pistachios.

Crabmeat Crackers

(40 crackers)

1 7-ounce can crabmeat, picked over
   carefully
4 tablespoons lemon juice
6 ounces cream cheese, softened
4 tablespoons heavy cream
4 tablespoons Mayonnaise
1 teaspoon minced onion
½ teaspoon Worcestershire sauce
2 drops Tabasco sauce

Mix the crabmeat with the lemon juice and let marinate for 1 hour. Combine all the other ingredients and add them to the crabmeat. Mound on crackers or melba rounds, spreading the mixture to the edges so the crackers will not burn. Broil, bake in a 400° oven until bubbly, or serve cold.

Hot Crab Dip

(2 cups)

1 7½-ounce can crabmeat, drained and
   picked over
1 8-ounce package cream cheese,
   softened
1 tablespoon horseradish
2 tablespoons cream
3 tablespoons chili sauce
Salt

Preheat the oven to 350°.
    Combine all the ingredients. Place in an ovenproof serving dish and bake for 15 minutes.

Antoine's Oysters Thermidor

(6 servings)

36 oysters on the half shell
3   cups Antoine's Cocktail Sauce
    (see below)
36 2-inch pieces of bacon

Preheat the oven to 400°.
    Place the oysters in a pan and bake until their edges begin to curl. Remove and cover

with the Cocktail Sauce. Top each oyster with a piece of bacon and return to the oven. Bake for 5 to 7 minutes more.

Antoine's Cocktail Sauce (3 cups):
- 4 tablespoons horseradish
- 3 tablespoons Worcestershire sauce
- 1 tablespoon Tabasco sauce
- ½ cup Antoine's Vinaigrette Sauce (*see below*)
- 2 cups ketchup
- ⅓ cup lemon juice

Blend all the ingredients and chill.

Antoine's Vinaigrette Sauce (1½ cups):
- ½ teaspoon salt
- ¼ teaspoon finely ground white pepper
- ½ teaspoon dry powdered mustard
- ⅓ cup vinegar
- 1 cup olive oil

Place all the ingredients in a bottle and shake to mix. Store at room temperature.

Jean Anderson's Baked Herring Appetizer
(Sill à la Tula Brettman)

(4–6 servings)
- 1 9-ounce jar herrings in wine, drained well
- 2 medium-sized leeks, trimmed, washed, and sliced thin
- ¼ cup chopped parsley
- ¼ cup freshly snipped dill
- 2 large hard-cooked eggs, peeled and finely chopped
- 2 tablespoons fine dry bread crumbs
- 3 tablespoons unsalted butter, melted

Preheat the oven to 350°.

In a buttered 9-inch pie pan layer the ingredients (sprinkling each successive layer over the preceding one as evenly as possible) in this order: the herring, leeks (separated into rings), parsley, dill, hard-cooked eggs, and finally the bread crumbs. Drizzle the melted butter evenly over all. Bake, uncovered, for 15 minutes. Spoon onto small plates and serve.

Anchovies & Roasted Red Peppers

(4 servings)

2–3 red peppers, washed well
⅓ cup olive oil
2 tablespoons lemon juice, or more to taste
1–2 cloves of garlic, crushed
Salt and freshly ground black pepper
Boston lettuce leaves *or* escarole, well washed and patted dry
1 small can whole anchovy fillets

Roast the peppers, whole, under the broiler, turning frequently, until the skins are blistered and charred. Let cool. Peel off the charred skin and cut the peppers into strips. Mix the olive oil and lemon juice in a bowl large enough to accommodate the pepper strips. Add the garlic and salt and pepper to taste. Add the pepper strips. Refrigerate for at least 2 hours, turning the pepper strips frequently in the marinade. When ready to serve, line four salad plates with the lettuce leaves and alternate the anchovy fillets and pepper strips in a circle, like the spokes of a wheel.

Smoked Salmon Soufflé

(4 servings)

¼ pound smoked salmon
7 tablespoons butter, softened
2 tablespoons chopped parsley *or* dill
4 tablespoons flour
1¾ cups milk
Salt and freshly ground black pepper
Nutmeg
4 eggs
1 egg white

Chop the salmon and mix in a small bowl with 2 tablespoons of softened butter and the parsley or dill. In a saucepan melt the remaining butter over low heat, add the flour, and cook for 1 minute. Add the milk, salt, pepper, and nutmeg and stir over low heat. When the sauce is thick, add the salmon.

Preheat the oven to 400°.

Separate the eggs and add the yolks to the salmon, one at a time. Beat the five egg whites until they form soft peaks and fold them gently into the salmon. Pour the mixture into a soufflé dish and bake for 30 minutes. Serve immediately.

Note: This dish will serve two as a luncheon or light supper dish.

Salmon Pâté

(2 cups)

1 15½-ounce can Red Sockeye salmon,
  drained well, bones and skin carefully
  removed
6 ounces cream cheese
3 tablespoons drained white horseradish
2 scallions (white part only)
1 tablespoon parsley
1 tablespoon lemon juice
2 drops Tabasco sauce
Few drops Worcestershire sauce

Place all the ingredients in the container of a
food processor fitted with the steel blade and
process until smooth. Chill for at least 1 hour
but preferably overnight, as the pâté is better
the second day. Serve on crackers or endive
leaves.

Egg & Sardine Spread

(1½ cups)

6 hard-cooked eggs
½ can sardines, drained
Dijon mustard
Mayonnaise
Minced parsley (garnish)

Mash the eggs and sardines and add the
mustard and mayonnaise to taste. (This is
easily done in a food processor.) Serve on
melba rounds, topped with the parsley.

Cheese-Sardine Ball

(8–10 servings)

1 can sardines
8 ounces cream cheese, softened
4 tablespoons capers, chopped
4 tablespoons parsley, chopped
2 tablespoons lemon juice
Salt to taste
Worcestershire sauce to taste
Paprika
Parsley (garnish)

Drain the oil from the sardines and mash them. Mix them with the cream cheese, capers, parsley, lemon juice, salt, and Worcestershire. Shape into a ball and chill. Serve sprinkled with the paprika and parsley and with thin pumpernickel rounds.

Bacon-wrapped Scallops

(60 bite-sized portions)

1 pound sea scallops, cut in bite-sized pieces
1 cup white wine
White pepper
½ pound bacon slices, cut in thirds

Place the scallops in a bowl with the wine and pepper to taste and marinate them for at least 30 minutes.

Preheat the oven to 375°.

Cook the bacon until it is soft but not crisp. Wrap the bacon pieces around the scallops and fasten them with toothpicks. Bake on a rack until the bacon is crisp. Serve warm.

Ceviche

(6–8 servings)

1 pound fresh bay scallops
1 cup fresh lemon juice *or* fresh lime juice
¼ cup chopped scallions
1 small can green chilies, chopped
10 cherry tomatoes, cut in half
¼ cup olive oil
2 tablespoons chopped parsley
Salt and freshly ground black pepper

In a bowl marinate the scallops in the lemon or lime juice for 3 or 4 hours. Drain. Add the remaining ingredients and toss. Season to taste. Let stand at least 1 more hour. Serve in scallop shells or on lettuce leaves.

Note: If using sea scallops slice them ¼ inch thick.

Variation: Ceviche can be made with any white fish cut into 1-inch cubes *or* with a combination of scallops and other fish.

Wolfgang Puck's Shrimp with Mustard
(Crevettes à la Moutarde)

(6 servings)

6–8 medium shrimp per person

Salt and freshly ground black pepper

4 tablespoons mild-flavored oil, such as almond or safflower

2 medium shallots, minced

1 bunch fresh tarragon, minced

½ cup dry sherry

½ cup heavy cream

½ pound unsalted butter, cut into small pieces

2 tablespoons Dijon mustard

1 tablespoon minced chives

Season the shrimp with the salt and pepper. Using two large sauté pans, heat the oil until it begins to smoke. Over very high heat, sauté the shrimp for 6 to 7 minutes. Transfer to a warm plate and keep warm. To each pan add 1 minced shallot and 1 tablespoon minced tarragon. Sauté for 2 to 3 minutes. Deglaze each pan with the sherry and then combine the sauce in one pan. Add the cream and reduce the sauce until it coats the back of a spoon. Whisk in the butter, one piece at a time. Whisk in the mustard at the last minute. Do not let the sauce boil or the mustard will become grainy. Correct the seasoning to taste. Arrange the shrimp decoratively on serving plates, nap with the sauce, and sprinkle with chives.

Note: This is the most requested appetizer at Ma Maison in Los Angeles. The shrimp will be crisp and succulent when sautéed over very high heat.

Helen Corbitt's Shrimp à la Helen

(2 dozen)

1 pound (20–25) shrimp, washed, peeled, and deveined

2 tablespoons finely minced parsley

2 cloves garlic, finely minced

1 cup olive or salad oil

Salt and freshly ground black pepper

Place the shrimp in a pan and cover with the other ingredients. Refrigerate all day — and overnight, too, if you have time. When ready to serve, place the shrimp on a shallow pan with the oil that clings to them and broil for 3 minutes on each side. Be sure not to overcook them or they will be tough and stringy. Season lightly with the salt and pepper. Spear with toothpicks to serve.

Note: These are good, too, when charcoal-broiled outside.

Donald Bruce White's Marinated Shrimp with Fresh Snow Peas

(20 pieces)

Marinade:

1	cup olive oil
⅓	cup wine *or* rice vinegar
¼	cup light soy sauce
1–2	teaspoons dry mustard, to taste
2	tablespoons fresh gingerroot, peeled and finely minced
1	clove garlic, peeled and finely minced

Grated zest of 1 or 2 oranges, to taste
Pinch of sugar
Salt and freshly ground black pepper

10	fresh or frozen snow peas
20	medium-small shrimp, cooked, peeled, and deveined

Combine all the marinade ingredients and adjust the seasoning as necessary. Reserve.

Blanch the fresh snow peas in salted boiling water for 1 minute only. Refresh under cold running water to stop the cooking and set the color. (If you are using frozen snow peas, simply thaw them.) Carefully split the snow peas, separating the two sides of the pods and discarding the tiny peas inside (or eat them as you work).

No more than 10 minutes before serving, toss the shrimp in the marinade (if you do this earlier, the soy will discolor the shrimp). Remove the shrimp immediately from the marinade and wrap half a snow pea across and around the shrimp. Secure with a toothpick and serve.

Note: This marinade can also be used to baste broiled fish or seafood.

Joan Itoh's Sweet-&-Sour Little Shrimps

(3 or 4 servings)

4½	ounces small canned shrimp *or* small shelled, cooked fresh shrimp
4	teaspoons sugar
4½	tablespoons vinegar
4½	teaspoons *shoyu*

If you are using canned shrimp, rinse them under cold water to remove the excess salt. In a bowl blend well the sugar, vinegar, and *shoyu*. Add the shrimp to the marinade and refrigerate for about 2 hours or overnight. Drain. Put 2 or 3 shrimps on a toothpick and place several on each plate or on a serving platter with other foods.

Note: Japanese *shoyu* and Chinese soy sauce differ a bit in flavor and texture. Only *shoyu* will give the desired results.

Marinated Shrimp

(10–12 servings)

- 1½ pounds raw shrimp, shelled and deveined
- 1 cup lime juice
- ½ cup chopped scallions
- 2 tablespoons chopped sweet red pepper (optional)

Salt and freshly ground black pepper

Cut the shrimp in half lengthwise, rinse, and pat dry. Mix in a bowl with the other ingredients and refrigerate for 4 hours or overnight. Taste for seasonings and adjust if necessary. Serve on toothpicks as an hors d'oeuvre or on lettuce leaves as a first course.

Tapenade

8–10 servings

- 1 can pitted black olives
- 10 anchovies
- 1 3½-ounce can tunafish
- 2 tablespoons capers
- ½ cup olive oil
- ¼ cup lemon juice

Using a food processor or blender purée the first 4 ingredients. Then add the oil and lemon juice a little at a time as in the procedure for preparing mayonnaise. Serve as a dip for raw vegetables or, as a first course, spooned over halved hard-cooked eggs.

Helen Corbitt's Pickled Shrimp

(25–30 pieces)

- 1 pound (25–30) shrimp, cooked and cleaned
- 2 tablespoons olive oil
- 1 cup vinegar
- 2 tablespoons water
- ¼ cup paper-thin slices of onion
- 8 whole cloves
- 1 bay leaf
- 2 teaspoons salt
- 1 teaspoon sugar

Dash of cayenne pepper

Place the shrimp in a pan and drizzle the oil over them. In a saucepan bring the rest of the ingredients to a boil and pour over the shrimp. Cool and refrigerate for at least 24 hours before serving.

Meat & Poultry

Hot Beef Dip

Sausage Pastry Balls

Cocktail Meatballs

Swedish Meatballs

Helen Corbitt's Meatballs

Donald Bruce White's Tiny Steak
    Tartare Balls

Cocktail Franks with Currant-Mustard
    Sauce

Cocktail Porcupine

Cocktail Hot Dogs

Salami or Bologna "Pies"

Toast Canapés

Ribbon Sandwiches

Parsleyed Ham (*Jambon Persillé*)

Ham & Asparagus Mornay

Ham Salad Puffs

Donald Bruce White's Fresh Figs with
    Prosciutto

Grilled Cheese & Ham Squares

Ham Rolls

Chicken Liver Roll

Chicken Liver Pâté

Molded Pâté

Helen Witty's Chicken Livers in
    Madeira

Rumaki

Olive-Bacon Rolls

Donald Bruce White's Skewered
    Smoked Turkey & Watermelon Rind

Hot Beef Dip

(6 servings)

    12 ounces cream cheese, softened
    1   2½-ounce jar chipped beef, finely
        chopped
    Horseradish

Preheat the oven to 350°.

In a bowl combine the ingredients and transfer to an ovenproof serving dish. Bake until bubbling, 10 to 15 minutes. Serve with large corn chips or toasted pita triangles.

Sausage Pastry Balls

(45 balls)

    1   pound sausage meat
    ½   pound extra sharp Cheddar cheese,
        grated
    2   cups quick biscuit mix *or* buttermilk-
        biscuit mix

Preheat the oven to 350°.

In a bowl combine the ingredients and mix well. Shape into walnut-sized balls. Bake on greased cookie sheets for 25 minutes. Serve hot.

Cocktail Meatballs

(50 meatballs)

Sauce:
    ½   cup minced onion
    1   teaspoon salt
    ½   teaspoon paprika
    1   teaspoon Dijon mustard
    5   tablespoons vinegar
    4   tablespoons brown sugar
    2   tablespoons Worcestershire sauce
    ½   cup lemon juice
    2½ cups chili sauce

Meatballs:
    3   pounds ground beef *or* 1 pound each
        beef, pork, and veal
    1   egg
    ¼   cup fresh white bread crumbs
    2   teaspoons Worcestershire sauce
    1¼ teaspoons salt
    Freshly ground black pepper
    1   tablespoon chopped parsley
    2   tablespoons butter or margarine

In a large skillet, sauté the chopped onion until brown and add the rest of the ingredients for the sauce. Simmer for 30 minutes.

Combine all the ingredients for the meatballs (except the butter), shape into balls, and brown them, a few at a time, in the butter.

(Don't overcook, as they will cook further in the sauce.)

Place the meatballs in the sauce and reheat. Serve from a chafing dish with toothpicks.

Swedish Meatballs

(4–6 servings)

½	cup dry bread crumbs
1¼	cups water
¾	pound ground beef
¼	pound ground pork
½	cup cold mashed potatoes
2	egg yolks
¾	cup cream
2	teaspoons salt
½	teaspoon white pepper
1½	tablespoons grated onion
3	tablespoons butter
2	tablespoons flour
1¾	cups beef stock or broth

Soak the bread crumbs in the water. In a large bowl combine all the other ingredients except the butter, flour, and stock or broth; then add the bread crumbs. Form the mixture into balls. Melt 2 tablespoons of the butter in a large skillet and brown the meatballs, turning frequently. Remove the balls from the pan and reserve.

Melt the remaining tablespoon of butter in the skillet. Add the 2 tablespoons flour and stir, browning the flour slightly. Remove from the heat and stir in the stock. Return the pan to the heat and stir the gravy until it has thickened. Add salt and pepper to taste. Cook over low heat for 5 to 10 minutes.

Return the meatballs to the sauce and heat them through. Serve from a chafing dish.

Variation: Form larger meatballs, and serve with egg noodles as a main course.

Helen Corbitt's Meatballs

(20 meatballs)

1 pound ground beef
1 small can Smithfield ham spread
Salt and freshly ground black pepper
Roquefort cheese
Dry red wine
Butter

In a bowl combine the ground beef and ham spread and season lightly with the salt and pepper. Cut pieces of Roquefort or another blue cheese into small squares and mold the meat around them. Place in a china or other nonmetallic bowl and add enough dry red wine to cover. Let stand in the refrigerator for at least 3 hours.

Melt a small amount of butter in a skillet, add a little of the wine from the meat, and pan-fry the meat patties to medium doneness. Serve from a hot platter or a chafing dish.

Donald Bruce White's Tiny Steak Tartare Balls

(20 meatballs)

½ pound sirloin steak (trimmed weight), free of all fat and gristle
Freshly ground black pepper
1–2 teaspoons cognac *or* brandy
1–2 teaspoons Worcestershire sauce
1–2 teaspoons Dijon mustard
¼ cup capers, drained and chopped
1 egg yolk
1 scallion, trimmed and chopped, including the green top
¼ cup finely chopped parsley, stems removed
2 tablespoons snipped chives, fresh *or* freeze-dried
20 thin pretzel sticks

Grind the trimmed meat in a food processor or grinder (or have your butcher grind it if you are sure the meat is completely free of fat before he begins). Mix the meat lightly with

the pepper (to taste), cognac, Worcestershire, mustard, capers, egg yolk, and scallion. Taste and adjust seasonings if necessary. Roll the meat into small balls about 1 inch in diameter.

In a small bowl or plate, combine the parsley and chives. Lightly roll the meatballs in the chopped herbs, shaking off any excess. Arrange the balls on a chilled platter and press the end of a small pretzel stick or toothpick into each to make a handle.

Cocktail Franks with Currant-Mustard Sauce

(10–12 servings)

1 10-ounce jar currant jelly
1 6-ounce jar yellow mustard
1 1-pound package cocktail frankfurters *or* regular frankfurters cut into pieces

Melt the jelly. Add the mustard and stir until smooth. Heat the frankfurters in the sauce and serve in a chafing dish with toothpicks.

Note: This sauce is excellent served cold with most cold meats. Try it with ham on a buffet table.

Cocktail Porcupine

(6–12 servings)

1	large round green cabbage
12–16	cocktail frankfurters, cooked
12–24	small shrimp, cooked, shelled, and deveined
12–16	small cubes Cheddar cheese *or* Swiss cheese
12–16	small cubes salami

Cut a slice from the bottom of the cabbage so that it will sit on a flat surface. Place on a round platter and pull down a few of the outer leaves to cover the platter. Place the frankfurters, shrimp, cheese, and salami cubes on toothpicks and push the picks into the cabbage.

Variations: This can also be done using a grapefruit or pineapple as the base. Garnish the platter with lettuce leaves for a more attractive presentation. Try cubes of ham on a pineapple, accompanied by a dish of Currant-Mustard Sauce.

Cocktail Hot Dogs

(10–12 servings)

¾	cup sherry
1½	cups ketchup
½	cup brown sugar
3	tablespoons A-1 sauce
1	pound cocktail hot dogs

In a small saucepan combine the first 4 ingredients. Bring to a boil and simmer for 15 minutes. Heat the hot dogs in the sauce. Serve from a chafing dish with toothpicks.

Salami or Bologna "Pies"

(6–8 servings)

8	ounces cream cheese, softened
½	pound salami *or* bologna, sliced thin

Spread the cheese evenly on the meat slices. Stack the slices 5 layers high, ending with the meat, and chill. Cut into pie-shaped wedges with a sharp knife. To serve, put a toothpick in each wedge.

Toast Canapés

(36 rounds)

> 9 pieces thin-sliced bread (white or other)
> Butter *or* Mayonnaise
> Toppings (see below)

Toast the bread. Using a small biscuit cutter or the top of a small drinking glass, cut 4 rounds from each piece of toast. Spread with butter or mayonnaise. Top with any combination of the following items that will appeal to the eye and the palate:

> ham and cheese or any cold meat and cheese
> sliced egg topped with an anchovy or watercress mayonnaise
> cream cheese and caviar or olives
> smoked salmon and capers or fresh dill
> peanut butter and bacon
> cottage cheese, scallions, and red pepper
> cucumber slices and dill
> cheese spread, liver pâté, or fish paste
> Roquefort butter and a walnut half

Ribbon Sandwiches

(8 finger sandwiches)

> Thin-sliced bread
> Deviled ham spread
> Cream cheese, softened
> Hard-cooked egg yolks moistened with Mayonnaise and mustard
> Watercress leaves, minced, mixed with softened butter

Cut crusts from thin-sliced bread. Spread one slice thinly with canned deviled ham, the next one with softened cream cheese, the next with hard-cooked egg yolk mixed with a little mayonnaise and mustard, and the fourth slice with minced watercress leaves mixed with softened butter. Make a 4-layered sandwich. Place in plastic wrap and chill for at least 1 hour. Cut into 8 small pieces with a very sharp knife.

Parsleyed Ham
(Jambon Persillé)

(8 servings)

2 pounds good-quality ham, trimmed of all fat
1 cup finely chopped parsley
1 envelope unflavored gelatin
¼ cup white wine *or* water
1 can consommé, diluted with water to make 2 cups
1 small clove garlic, crushed (optional)
Freshly ground black pepper

Cut the ham into julienne pieces. Combine the ham and the parsley and place in a loaf pan or mold. Sprinkle the gelatin on the wine or water and let it soften for 5 minutes. Heat the consommé, and add the gelatin mixture, garlic if desired, and pepper to taste. Stir until the gelatin is completely dissolved. When the mixture is cool and syrupy, spoon over the ham mixture and chill until firm. Unmold, slice, and serve with mustard and *cornichons.*

Note: Imported canned ham is excellent for this recipe.

Ham & Asparagus Mornay

(6 servings)

36 fresh asparagus spears
6 slices boiled ham
1 cup Mornay Sauce
Grated Gruyère cheese

Preheat the oven to 375°.

Clean the asparagus and cook until just tender. Drain well and place on a towel to absorb all liquid. Prepare the Mornay Sauce. Roll 6 asparagus spears in each ham slice and place the rolls close together in a baking dish, seam side down. Cover with the sauce and sprinkle with the cheese. Bake for 15 to 20 minutes. Serve hot.

Notes: This recipe can be prepared ahead of time and covered with plastic wrap, then baked just before serving.

This delicious first course can be a wonderful main course for lunch or dinner. Serve 2 rolls to each person for a main course.

Ham Salad Puffs

(20 puffs)

Filling:
- 1   cup chopped, cooked ham
- ½   cup chopped celery
- ¼   cup chopped green pepper
- 1'   teaspoon minced onion
- 2–3 tablespoons Mayonnaise
- 2   teaspoons Sloe Gin (optional)

Ham Salad Puffs:
- ¼ cup butter, softened
- ½ cup water
- ½ cup flour
- ⅛ teaspoon salt
- Dash of cayenne pepper (optional)
- 2 eggs

In a small bowl combine all the filling ingredients and stir gently with a wooden spoon. Cover and refrigerate.

Preheat the oven to 400°.

Bring the butter and water to a boil in a small saucepan (the butter should be melted). Remove from the heat and add the flour, salt, and cayenne all at once, stirring to combine. Place over low heat and continue stirring until the dough leaves the sides of the pan and forms a ball. Remove from the heat and add the eggs, one at a time, beating well after each addition. Drop the dough by rounded teaspoonfuls on a cookie sheet, 2 inches apart. Bake for 25 minutes, or until puffed and nicely browned. Cool on a wire rack.

To serve, remove the top of each puff with a sharp paring knife, fill with a rounded tablespoon of the filling, and replace the top.

Donald Bruce White's Fresh Figs with Prosciutto

(20 pieces)

- 5 ripe figs, peeled
- Juice of 1 fresh lime
- 5 slices of prosciutto (imported or domestic)
- Fresh lime wedges (garnish)

Shortly before serving, quarter the figs and sprinkle them with lime juice to prevent discoloration. Cut each ham slice crosswise into 4 pieces. Wrap a piece around each fig section, fastening it with a toothpick, if desired. Garnish with wedges of fresh lime.

Grilled Cheese & Ham Squares

(16 squares)

8 slices thin white bread
4 slices Swiss cheese
4 slices boiled ham
Softened butter

Preheat the oven to 375°.

Place a slice of the ham and a slice of the cheese on each of 4 pieces of the bread. Cover with the remaining bread. Remove the crusts, butter the outsides of the sandwiches, and cut into fourths. Place on a cookie sheet and bake until golden. Serve hot.

Ham Rolls

(20 rolls)

6 ounces cream cheese, softened
2 tablespoons horseradish (or to taste)
1 tablespoon cream
5 slices boiled ham
1 jar small sour pickles (French *cornichons*)

In a bowl combine the cheese, horseradish, and cream and spread evenly on the ham. Cut the rounded ends off the pickles and place the pickles end to end lengthwise 1 inch inside the left edge of the coated ham slices. Fold each edge over the pickles and roll tightly. Chill; cut into bite-sized pieces. Serve on toothpicks.

Variations: This can also be done using roast beef, dried beef, corned beef, or salami.

Chicken Liver Roll

(16 servings)

- 1 pound chicken livers
- 1 medium onion, grated
- 4 hard-boiled eggs, chopped
- ½ cup Mayonnaise
- Salt and freshly ground black pepper
- Chopped parsley

In a saucepan cover the livers with boiling water and cook for 5 minutes. Drain the livers and add the onion, eggs, mayonnaise, and salt and pepper to taste. Chop in a blender or a food processor. Shape into a ball and roll in the chopped parsley. Serve surrounded by toast or melba rounds.

Chicken Liver Pâté

(12 servings)

- 4 tablespoons butter
- 4 shallots, minced
- 1 pound chicken livers, well cleaned and drained
- ¼ cup brandy
- ¼ cup heavy cream
- 2 tablespoons minced parsley
- Salt and freshly ground black pepper

In a medium-size skillet melt the butter and cook the shallots until they are soft but not brown. Add the livers and cook for 5 minutes. Add the brandy and ignite. Add the cream and salt and pepper to taste. Purée with the parsley in a food processor or a blender (the mixture will be very liquid). Pour into a serving dish, cover with plastic wrap, and chill. This pâté is better the second day and will keep for a week. Serve on melba toast.

Molded Pâté

(8–10 servings)

1 package unflavored gelatin
2 tablespoons cold water
1 10½-ounce can consommé
Sliced olives (optional)
Pimiento (optional)
Hard-cooked egg whites (optional)
Lightly steamed carrot slices (optional)
1 4-ounce can liver pâté *or* 4 ounces
   liverwurst
1 3½-ounce package cream cheese,
   softened
2 tablespoons brandy

In a small bowl sprinkle the gelatin on the cold water and let stand for 5 minutes. Heat the consommé and add the softened gelatin, stirring until it has dissolved. Oil a 3- or 4-cup mold lightly. Pour the gelatin into the mold to a depth of ½ inch and chill until firm (this is quickly done in the freezer). If you wish to decorate your mold, do so with the sliced olives, pimiento, bits of egg white, and the carrot slices. "Glue" them down with a little of the gelatin. Chill again until firm.

Blend the liver pâté and cream cheese well and add the brandy. Add the pâté to the mold, leaving some space at the edge for the rest of the gelatin. Gently pour the remaining gelatin into the mold and chill until firm. Unmold and serve with melba rounds.

Helen Witty's Chicken Livers in Madeira

(3 servings)

¾ pound chicken livers
Salt and freshly ground black pepper
Flour for dusting livers
4 tablespoons (½ stick) butter
2 tablespoons vegetable oil
½ cup Madeira
Few drops lemon juice (optional)
2 tablespoons thin scallion rounds,
   including green tops (garnish)

Halve the livers and trim off any fat or stringy bits. Pat the livers dry on paper towels.

Just before cooking, dry the livers again and season them with the salt and pepper. Roll them well in the flour, shaking off any excess. Heat the butter and oil together in a large skillet over medium-high heat. When the foam of the butter dies down, add the livers, shaking the pan and turning them so they brown quickly on all sides, about 5 minutes. They should still be pink inside.

Transfer the livers to a warm dish, leaving the juices behind. Add the Madeira to the pan. Swirl over high heat for a minute or two, until the sauce reduces a little, then return the livers to the pan and swirl them briefly in the sauce. Check the seasoning, adding the lemon juice as well as salt and pepper, if you like. Serve immediately on small plates or spear with toothpicks.

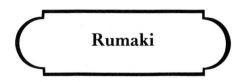

Rumaki

(2 dozen)

6 chicken livers, cut in quarters
24 canned water chestnuts, drained
12 slices bacon, cut in half
½ cup soy sauce
¼ cup sherry
1 teaspoon minced fresh *or* ½ teaspoon dry ginger

Wrap a water chestnut and a chicken liver quarter in each half-slice of bacon and secure with a toothpick. Combine the remaining ingredients and marinate the rumaki in this sauce for at least 1 hour.

Preheat the oven to 400°.

Place the rumaki on a rack in a baking pan and bake until the bacon is crisp, 15 to 20 minutes. Serve hot.

Olive-Bacon Rolls

(18 rolls)

18 large stuffed green olives
6 slices bacon, cut in thirds

Preheat the oven to 450°.

Wrap the bacon pieces around the olives and secure them with toothpicks. Bake or broil on a rack until the bacon is crisp, 6 to 10 minutes. Drain on paper towels and serve immediately.

Donald Bruce White's Skewered Smoked Turkey & Watermelon Rind

(2 dozen)

¼ pound smoked turkey breast, sliced ½ inch thick
1 10-ounce jar pickled watermelon rind, drained
Small wooden skewers or cocktail picks

Cut the turkey and watermelon rind into uniform ½-inch cubes. Alternately thread the turkey and watermelon rind cubes onto the picks, leaving an end of each skewer to serve as a handle. Arrange the skewers on a serving platter.

Note: The skewers may be covered and refrigerated until serving time.

Vegetable Appetizers

Curry Dip
Lo-Cal Dip
Dill Sauce
Crudité Plate
Antipasto Salad
Artichokes Ravigote
Donald Bruce White's Arugula-
    Watercress Canapés
Guacamole
Avocado Mold
Michael Batterberry's Cauliflower with
    Mustard Seed Butter
Cabbage Vegetable Platter
Marinated Broccoli
Celery Rémoulade
Cucumber Cups
Stuffed Cucumber Canapés
Hummus
Baked Grapefruit with Sherry
Michael Batterberry's Lentil Salad
Mushrooms à la Grecque
Elizabeth Esterling's Artichokes with
    Mushrooms in Tomato Cream

Michael Batterberry's Fresh Pickled
    Mushrooms
Richard Sax's Mushrooms Stuffed with
    Garlic Cream Cheese
Richard Sax's Sausage-stuffed Hot
    Mushrooms
Hot Mushroom Rolls
Marinated Mushrooms
Joan Itoh's Pickled Japanese
    Mushrooms
Stuffed Mushrooms
Toasted Mushroom Sandwiches
Spinach-stuffed Mushrooms
Baked Onion Dip
Onion Toasts
Richard Lavin's String Bean Salad
Filled Cherry Tomatoes
Fancy Tomatoes
Helen Corbitt's Texas Caviar
Spinach Balls
Zucchini Squares

Curry Dip

(1¼ cups)

1 cup Mayonnaise
1 teaspoon lemon juice
1 teaspoon curry powder
½ teaspoon minced onion
½ teaspoon Worcestershire sauce
¼ cup chili sauce
Salt and freshly ground black pepper

Combine all the ingredients with a whisk or in a food processor or blender. Serve with raw or lightly steamed vegetables.

Dill Sauce

(1½ cups)

⅔ cup Mayonnaise
⅔ cup sour cream
2 tablespoons minced scallions
2 tablespoons minced dill
2 tablespoons minced parsley
Salt and freshly ground black pepper to taste

Combine all the ingredients with a whisk or in a blender or food processor. This makes an excellent dip for shrimp or raw vegetables.

Lo-Cal Dip

(2½ cups)

1 pound low-fat cottage cheese
Mustard (to taste)
Horseradish (to taste)
2 tablespoons minced parsley
½ cup low-fat yogurt

Combine all the ingredients except the yogurt in a food processor or blender for a smooth dip. Stir in the yogurt. Serve with raw vegetables.

Crudité Plate

A popular first course in France is a combination of any four of the following salads served on individual plates.

Celery Rémoulade
Lentil Salad
Marinated Mushrooms
String Bean Salad
Grated carrots
Artichoke hearts
Sliced beets, drained
Cucumber salad
Potatoes vinaigrette

Antipasto Salad

(4 servings)

1 sweet red pepper
2 cups canned chickpeas
1 small can pitted ripe olives
½ pound pepperoni, sliced thin
2 tablespoons capers
2 tablespoons chopped parsley
½ teaspoon fennel seeds
1 cup Vinaigrette, with garlic
Chopped parsley

Cut the pepper into small pieces. Blanch them in boiling water for 1 minute and refresh them under cold water, to keep their color. In a salad bowl, mix the pepper pieces with all the other ingredients and toss well to coat with the vinaigrette. Allow the salad to marinate for 1 hour before serving. Serve on lettuce leaves and garnish with additional chopped parsley.

Artichokes Ravigote

(6 servings)

- 6 globe artichokes
- ½ lemon

Sauce Ravigote:
- 1 cup Vinaigrette with mustard
- 3 shallots, *or* white part of scallions
- 1 tablespoon capers
- 1 tablespoon parsley
- ¼ teaspoon dried tarragon
- ¼ teaspoon dried chervil
- 2 tablespoons Mayonnaise

With a serrated knife, cut off the stems and 1 inch from the tops of the artichokes. With scissors, cut the sharp tips from the leaves. Rub the bottoms with the lemon to prevent discoloration. Place the artichokes in a large saucepan. Cover them with water and simmer for 30 to 45 minutes, or until the bottom of an artichoke is tender when pierced with a fork. Turn upside down to drain and cool. Spread the leaves and remove the choke, using a spoon or melon baller.

Prepare the sauce by placing all the ingredients in a blender or food processor and puréeing. Spoon the sauce into the center of the artichokes.

Donald Bruce White's Arugula-Watercress Canapés

(12–16 canapés)

- ½ bunch fresh arugula (rocket)
- ½ bunch fresh watercress (*or* use all watercress)
- ½ small white onion, grated (about 1½ tablespoons)
- Dash of Tabasco or other hot pepper sauce
- Salt
- 1 tablespoon lemon juice
- 1–2 tablespoons Mayonnaise, preferably homemade
- 4–8 slices firm white bread

Remove the coarse stems from the arugula and the watercress. Rinse the sprigs quickly in cold water; squeeze carefully to remove all excess moisture. Chop fine and place in a bowl. Add the onion, Tabasco, salt to taste, lemon juice, and just enough mayonnaise to hold the mixture together. Reserve.

Toast the bread until golden and slightly crisp. While the toast is hot, use a biscuit cutter or a glass to cut 2 to 4 rounds (depending on the size of the cutter) from each slice. Place the rounds on a rack until needed (to prevent their becoming soggy).

To serve, mound the filling on the toast rounds with a teaspoon. (You may want to reheat the toast in a 375° oven.)

Note: Arugula is a strongly flavored, dark green member of the leaf lettuce family, widely used in Italy for salads and available here from many greengrocers.

Guacamole

(16 servings)

2   medium-sized ripe tomatoes
2   ripe avocados
⅓   cup lemon juice
5   scallions, minced, including green tops
2   tablespoons Mayonnaise
1   small clove garlic, crushed (optional)
Tabasco sauce
Salt

Drop the tomatoes into boiling water for 1 minute, cool under running water, and peel. Cut the tomatoes in half, scoop out the seeds and the jelly, and chop the tomato flesh finely. Mash the avocados with a stainless steel fork and combine with the tomatoes and the remaining ingredients. Taste for seasonings; guacamole should be quite spicy. Cover with plastic wrap, as it darkens easily. Serve with tortilla chips.

Note: To prevent darkening, put the avocado pit in the guacamole until ready to serve.

Avocado Mold

(8 servings)

1   envelope unflavored gelatin
¼   cup cold water
1   cup chicken broth, heated
2   tablespoons lemon juice
1   tablespoon horseradish
1   teaspoon onion juice
¼   teaspoon curry powder
¼   teaspoon dried tarragon, crushed
Salt
Cayenne pepper
½   cup heavy cream, whipped
½   cup Mayonnaise
1   ripe avocado, mashed
Cherry tomatoes (garnish)
Pitted black olives (garnish)

Sprinkle the gelatin in the water in a small dish, let stand for 5 minutes, then dissolve it completely in the broth. Add the lemon juice, horseradish, onion juice, curry, tarragon, and salt and cayenne to taste. Chill until syrupy. In a bowl mix with the whipped cream, mayonnaise, and avocado. Pour into a 4-cup ring mold and chill. Unmold onto a bed of lettuce, and fill the center with cherry tomatoes and black olives.

Michael Batterberry's Cauliflower with Mustard Seed Butter

(4–6 servings)

- 1 medium head cauliflower
- ½ lemon
- 1 tablespoon plus 1 teaspoon coarse salt
- 2 cups unflavored yogurt
- 3 tablespoons mustard seeds
- 5 tablespoons clarified butter

Cut the cauliflower into medium-sized florets and trim the heavy skin from their stems with a sharp knife. Place the florets in a large enamel pan with cold water barely to cover, and add the juice of the ½ lemon. Bring to a boil, sprinkle with a tablespoon of the coarse salt, and simmer for 4 to 5 minutes. Refresh the florets under cold water and drain thoroughly. Beat the yogurt with the teaspoon of salt until smooth and creamy. Toss the cooled, dry cauliflower in the yogurt and refrigerate.

In a small, heavy, enamel cast-iron pot with a cover, fry the mustard seeds over high heat in the clarified butter. When you begin to hear popping and spattering sounds, count to 50 and remove the pan from the heat. Do not lift the lid for another 5 minutes. In a serving bowl, drizzle the mustard seed butter over the cauliflower and yogurt, and swirl to-gether lightly with a wooden spoon. Do not overmix; this *raita* should have a streaky appearance. Serve with toothpicks for spearing.

Cabbage Vegetable Platter

(6–12 servings)

- 1 small, attractive head of red *or* green cabbage
- 1½ cups Russian dressing
- 1 bunch broccoli, florets only, raw *or* lightly steamed
- 1 head cauliflower, florets only, raw *or* lightly steamed

Cut a slice from the bottom of the cabbage so that it will sit on a plate. Scoop out the center of the cabbage and reserve it for another use. Place the hollow cabbage on a platter and fill the cavity with the Russian dressing. Surround it with the broccoli and cauliflower florets.

Marinated Broccoli

(10 servings)

1 bunch broccoli, very fresh
1 8-ounce bottle Italian salad dressing *or*
1 cup of your own Italian dressing

Cut the broccoli into florets and marinate in the dressing overnight. Serve with toothpicks.

Celery Rémoulade

(6 servings)

1   pound celery root
1½ teaspoons salt
1½ teaspoons lemon juice
2   tablespoons Dijon mustard
3   tablespoons boiling water
½   cup corn oil
2   tablespoons vinegar
Salt and freshly ground black pepper
Chopped parsley (garnish)

Peel the celery and cut into julienne pieces. (This is quickly done in the food processor with the shredding blade.) Put the celery in a bowl and toss it with the salt and the lemon juice. Let it stand for 30 minutes to soften the celery and remove any bitter taste. Rinse, and dry the celery with a dish towel.

Place the mustard in a warmed bowl. Using a whisk, beat in, bit by bit, first the boiling water and then the oil. The mixture should be creamy. Gradually add the vinegar; season to taste.

Toss the celery with the dressing and let marinate for 2 to 3 hours or overnight. Serve on lettuce leaves, sprinkled with the chopped parsley.

Variation: Substitute a mustard-flavored Mayonnaise for the dressing.

Cucumber Cups

(8–12 servings)

2 long thin cucumbers, peeled

Score the cucumbers lengthwise with the tines of a fork and cut into ¾-inch pieces. With a melon baller, scoop out the center portion, leaving ¼ inch at the bottom to form the cup. Fill with Salmon Pâté, shrimp spread, or your choice of filling.

Note: These can be filled attractively by using a pastry bag.

Stuffed Cucumber Canapés

(40 canapés)

2 long, narrow cucumbers, peeled, ends trimmed
4 ounces cream cheese
2 tablespoons Worcestershire sauce
1 teaspoon garlic salt *or* more to taste
Flat round crackers

Run the tines of a fork down the sides of the peeled cucumbers to score them attractively. With an apple corer or small, sharp, thin-bladed knife, remove the seeds from the cucumber. In a small bowl blend the cream cheese with the Worcestershire sauce and garlic salt. Pack the cream cheese mixture into the cucumber hollows and chill the cucumbers well. Cut the cucumbers into thin slices and place the rounds on the crackers just before serving.

Hummus

(10 servings)

1 pound dry chickpeas, picked over and washed
1 cup corn oil *or* ¾ cup corn oil and ¼ cup olive oil
1 clove garlic, minced
1 teaspoon salt
Few grains cayenne pepper
3 teaspoons lemon juice

In a large saucepan cover the chickpeas with water. Bring to a boil, remove from the heat, and let soak for 1 hour. Drain and cover with fresh water. Bring to a boil and simmer until very soft, about 2 hours. Drain.

Combine the chickpeas with the rest of the ingredients in a blender or food processor and purée. Use as a spread or dip.

Note: Hummus is especially good served on pita bread.

Baked Grapefruit with Sherry

½ grapefruit per person, sectioned, seeds removed
Sherry

Preheat the oven to 350°.

Place the grapefruit halves in a baking dish. Sprinkle each half with 1 teaspoon sherry and bake for 20 minutes. Serve warm.

Note: If possible, let the grapefruit marinate in the sherry for 1 hour before cooking.

Michael Batterberry's Lentil Salad

(12–16 servings)

1 pound lentils
2 carrots, scraped
2 bay leaves
1 teaspoon thyme
1 tablespoon plus 1½ teaspoons coarse salt
6 tablespoons high-quality olive oil
1½ teaspoons dry mustard
6 grindings of black pepper from a pepper mill
1 teaspoon ground coriander
1 clove garlic, crushed
2 tablespoons red wine vinegar
½ medium-sized red onion, finely chopped
1 cup chopped celery
Sprigs of watercress (garnish)
Cherry tomatoes (garnish)
Greek olives (garnish)

In a saucepan cook the lentils in water to cover by at least 1½ inches along with the carrots, bay leaves, and thyme. When tender but not mushy, season with 1 tablespoon of the salt, cook 1 minute more, and drain in a colander. Remove the carrots and reserve them. (Cooking time will vary anywhere from 18 to 25 minutes.)

Prepare a dressing by mixing the olive oil into a paste with the dry mustard, the remaining salt, the pepper, coriander, garlic, and vinegar. While the lentils are still warm, toss them in the dressing, taking care not to mash them. Dice the carrots and stir them, the onion, and the celery into the lentils. Marinate the mixture at room temperature for at least 2 hours. Taste for seasonings and add more salt and pepper if desired. Serve on salad plates, garnished with the watercress, cherry tomatoes, and olives.

Notes: Capers are extremely compatible as an additional garnish.

This recipe may be halved.

Variation: To serve as a salad, mound the lentils into a low dome on a plate or platter and decorate with very thin slices of red onion (well rinsed under cold running water, dried with paper towels, and dressed with lemon juice), and sprinkle liberally with chopped fresh parsley.

Mushrooms à la Grecque

(4 servings)

    1   cup water
    ½   cup olive oil
    6   peppercorns
   12   coriander seeds
    1   bay leaf
    ¼   teaspoon dried thyme
    ¼   teaspoon salt
    1   pound button mushrooms
   Lemon juice

In a saucepan combine all the ingredients except the mushrooms and lemon juice. Bring to a boil and simmer for 5 minutes. Rinse the mushrooms, wipe dry, and cut the bottoms from the stems. Rub the mushrooms with the lemon juice and add them to the simmering liquid. Let it return to the boil and simmer for about 5 more minutes. Let the mushrooms cool in the liquid. Serve on lettuce leaves.

Note: If small mushrooms are not available, cut larger ones in quarters.

Variation: Other vegetables can be prepared in the same manner, but you will have to adjust the cooking time to suit each one. Vegetables à la Grecque should always be tender but firm.

Elizabeth Esterling's
Artichokes with Mushrooms
in Tomato Cream

(6 servings)

1 cup Mayonnaise
1 cup sour cream
1 tablespoon dry sherry
2 tablespoons lemon juice
½ teaspoon Tabasco sauce
3 tablespoons tomato paste
Salt and freshly ground black pepper
1 pound mushrooms, washed, dried, and sliced
6 large artichoke bottoms, cooked (fresh *or* canned)
Chopped parsley (garnish)

In a bowl combine all the ingredients except the artichokes and the parsley and stir well. Serve over the artichoke bottoms and garnish with the parsley. (If you are using canned artichoke bottoms, drain well before serving.)

Note: If the artichoke bottoms are small, allow two per person.

Michael Batterberry's
Fresh Pickled Mushrooms

(10–12 servings)

1½ pounds firm white mushrooms
1½ cups red wine vinegar
¾ cup brown sugar
1 cup water
6–8 large garlic cloves, peeled and split lengthwise
2½ teaspoons coarse salt
6 bay leaves
14 peppercorns
2 cloves
1 teaspoon thyme
3 slices lemon
¼ cup olive oil plus a few extra teaspoons
Lemon wedges (garnish)

Wipe the mushrooms clean with a cloth or damp paper towel, and trim the bottoms from the stems. If the mushrooms are large, cut them into two, three, or four pieces, remembering that they will shrink in pickling to approximately half of their original volume. In a wide enamel pot simmer all the other ingredients (except the extra olive oil) for 15 minutes. Gently drop in the mushrooms and cook, stirring gently, for 3 or 4 minutes, until all the mushrooms are flavored with the pungent juices. Remove from the heat and allow the mushrooms to cool in the juices, turning them gently every so often with a spoon. Remove the mushrooms from the juice with a slotted spoon, let drain briefly, and toss before serving with just enough olive oil to coat them slightly. Arrange the mushrooms on a platter and decorate with the lemon wedges and the bay leaves from the pot.

Note: Strain the juices and keep for pickling the next batch of mushrooms. (The liquid will keep in the refrigerator for at least 2 weeks.)

Richard Sax's Mushrooms Stuffed with Garlic Cream Cheese

(16 mushrooms)

    16 medium-sized fresh mushrooms, well
        wiped
    Fresh lemon juice
    1   5-ounce package garlic cream cheese
        (Boursin type), at room temperature
    1   teaspoon chopped parsley *or* snipped
        chives (garnish)

Remove the stems from the mushrooms and mince them. Sprinkle the caps with the lemon juice to prevent discoloration. Beat the cheese in a small bowl until it is fluffy; add the chopped mushroom stems. Using a pastry bag or a spoon, fill the mushroom caps with the cheese mixture. Garnish with the parsley or chives. Serve cold.

Richard Sax's Sausage-stuffed Hot Mushrooms

(16 mushrooms)

    16 medium-sized fresh mushrooms,
        well wiped
    Fresh lemon juice
    ½   pound sweet Italian sausage
    Salt and freshly ground black pepper
    1   tablespoon butter
    1   teaspoon chopped parsley (garnish)

Remove the stems from the mushrooms and mince them. Sprinkle the caps with the lemon juice to prevent discoloration. Remove the sausage meat from its casings and place it in a large bowl. Add the minced mushroom stems and a small amount of salt and pepper. Blend thoroughly, using a light touch.

Preheat the oven to 375°.

Grease a baking dish with the butter. Spoon the sausage mixture into the mushroom caps, smoothing the tops into a rounded shape, and place in the baking dish, sausage side up. Bake about 15 minutes, until the sausage meat is cooked through. Serve hot, garnished with the parsley.

Hot Mushroom Rolls

(32 pieces)

Duxelles:

4	tablespoons butter
2	shallots, finely chopped
½	pound mushrooms with stems, finely minced

Salt and freshly ground black pepper

8	thin slices white bread, with crusts removed

Melted butter

In a medium-size skillet melt the butter and cook the shallots until they are soft but not brown. Place the minced mushrooms in a dish towel and squeeze out their juice, then add to the shallots and cook over high heat until the moisture has evaporated and the mushrooms are dark brown. Season to taste with the salt and pepper.

With a rolling pin, flatten the bread slices (they will be easier to roll). Spread the bread with a fine layer of the duxelles and roll up each slice jelly roll fashion. With a pastry brush, spread the melted butter over the rolls. Chill or freeze them to make them easier to cut.

Preheat the oven to 350°.

Cut each roll into 4 bite-size pieces and bake until golden, about 10 minutes.

Notes: A food processor does an excellent job of mincing the mushrooms.

Duxelles may be refrigerated in a jar or frozen in small portions. They can be added to soups, sauces, omelettes — whenever you want a mushroom flavor.

Variation: To serve cold, spread the flattened bread with softened cream cheese and a thin layer of duxelles. Roll, chill, and cut.

Marinated Mushrooms

(6 servings)

½	cup olive oil
3	tablespoons lemon juice
½	teaspoon dried oregano, crushed
½	teaspoon salt

Freshly ground black pepper

½	pound fresh mushrooms, sliced

Combine the first 5 ingredients and toss with the mushrooms. Let marinate from 1 to 24 hours. Serve as an hors d'oeuvre on toothpicks or on lettuce leaves as a first course.

Joan Itoh's Pickled Japanese Mushrooms

(6 servings)

12 dried *shiitake* mushrooms
½ cup *dashi or* stock
4 tablespoons sugar
4 tablespoons *shoyu*
1 teaspoon *mirin* (sweet sake)
1 teaspoon sake

Soak the mushrooms in water for 15 minutes to soften. Remove the stems. Boil the caps in the *dashi* or stock for 10 to 12 minutes. Add the sugar, stir, reduce the heat, and continue simmering for 15 minutes. Add the *shoyu* and cook for 10 more minutes; then blend in the *mirin* and sake and simmer gently until the pan juices are reduced to a thick syrup. Serve cold in little dishes.

Note: Mirin is an especially sweet sake, used mainly for cooking. Though sake itself, like other wines, comes both dry and sweet, *mirin* is quite a bit stronger, and a little goes a long way.

Variation: The flavor and appearance of these mushrooms is a little different when sprinkled with white sesame seeds.

Stuffed Mushrooms

(50 mushrooms)

50 bite-size mushrooms
2 tablespoons minced onion
4 tablespoons butter
½ cup herb stuffing mix
1 tablespoon chopped parsley
Salt and freshly ground black pepper

Preheat the oven to 350°.

Rinse the mushrooms and wipe dry. Remove the stems and mince them. In a saucepan cook the onion in the butter until it is soft. Add the chopped stems. Then add the stuffing mix and parsley and season with the salt and pepper. Fill the mushroom caps with the mixture and place them in a baking pan just large enough to hold them. Pour in a thin layer of water and bake for 15 minutes. Serve hot.

Toasted Mushroom Sandwiches

(16 pieces)

2 tablespoons flour
¼ cup dry sherry or vermouth
¾ pound raw mushrooms, chopped
1 10½-ounce can mushroom soup
Salt and freshly ground black pepper
Worcestershire sauce
Tabasco sauce
8 thin slices white bread
Butter, softened

In a saucepan mix the flour and sherry and add the mushrooms and the soup. Add the seasonings to taste and cook over low heat for 10 minutes, stirring constantly. Refrigerate until the mixture is thick enough to spread.

Preheat the oven to 325°.

Trim the crusts from the bread and make sandwiches using the mushroom spread. Butter the outsides of the bread. Cut each sandwich into fourths and bake until golden brown.

Note: This mixture can be served in prebaked tart shells as a first course or luncheon dish.

Spinach-stuffed Mushrooms

(12–16 servings)

2 pounds medium-sized mushrooms, cleaned, stems removed
1 package frozen spinach soufflé, defrosted
½ pound Swiss cheese, sliced thin

Preheat the oven to 375°.

Fill the mushroom caps with the spinach soufflé and cover each one with a small piece of the cheese. Place in a baking dish and pour in ½ cup of water. Bake for 20 to 25 minutes. Drain on paper towels before serving on small plates or from a large platter.

Note: The pieces of cheese should be smaller than the mushrooms so the melted cheese doesn't drip over the sides. If you wish, you can use grated cheese.

Baked Onion Dip

(2 cups)

1 medium onion, minced
1 cup coarsely grated sharp Cheddar
   cheese
1 cup Mayonnaise

Preheat the oven to 400°.

In a bowl combine all the ingredients. Place the mixture in an ovenproof serving dish and bake for 20 minutes. Serve with large corn chips or toasted pita triangles.

Onion Toasts

(36–48 fingers)

½ pound butter, softened
1 envelope onion soup mix
1 loaf thinly sliced white bread, crusts
   removed

Preheat the oven to 325°.

In a bowl combine the butter and the soup mix and spread on the bread. Cut into fingers and bake for 15 minutes.

Note: Whole slices may be frozen before cooking. Cut; bake directly from the freezer for 18 minutes in a 325° oven.

Richard Lavin's String Bean Salad

(4–6 servings)

    1 pound string beans, thoroughly
       cleaned and washed
    ¼ cup grated radish
    3 tablespoons Vinaigrette
       Salt and freshly ground black pepper

Blanch the string beans in vigorously boiling water for approximately 1 minute, remove immediately, and place in ice water. Do not overcook. Drain the beans when they are cool. Mix the beans with the radish, toss with the vinaigrette, and add salt and pepper to taste. Serve on salad plates.

Note: Radishes can be grated easily and quickly with a food processor.

Filled Cherry Tomatoes

(8–12 servings)

    1 carton firm cherry tomatoes
       Cream cheese and chives *or* Boursin
       cheese *or* tuna *or* shrimp salad

Cut the tops off the cherry tomatoes and remove the seeds with a tiny spoon or melon baller. Turn upside down on a paper towel to drain. Fill the tomato cases with the cheese, softened, or with a salad.

Note: These can be filled attractively using a pastry bag.

Fancy Tomatoes

(6 servings)

    6   medium tomatoes, ripe but still
         firm
    1–2 hard-cooked eggs, sliced
    1–2 medium red onions, sliced
    1   cucumber, peeled, trimmed, and
         sliced
    6   large, attractive lettuce leaves

Turn the tomatoes upside down and make a series of vertical cuts without slicing through the tomato. Insert the egg, onion, and cucumber slices into the cuts gently. Place the tomatoes on salad plates lined with the lettuce leaves. Serve with your favorite salad dressing.

Helen Corbitt's Texas Caviar

(6–8 servings)

2   20-ounce cans black-eyed peas
1   cup salad oil
¼   cup wine vinegar
1   clove garlic *or* garlic seasoning
¼   cup thinly sliced onion
½   teaspoon salt
Cracked or freshly ground black pepper

Drain the peas and place them in a pan or bowl. Add the remaining ingredients and mix thoroughly. Refrigerate in a jar. Remove the garlic after 1 day. Store for at least 2 days and up to 2 weeks before eating. (You'll need a plate and fork for these.)

Note: In the South, the black-eyed pea is the traditional good-luck food for New Year's Day, and a good Texan eats them sometime during the day to ensure prosperity for the coming year — whether he likes them or not. I came to Texas wide-eyed and innocent about such shenanigans — and I didn't like the peas, either. So-o-o, I pickled them. Since then I have few parties at any time of the year without them.

Variations: Red kidney beans and garbanzos work equally well in this recipe.

Spinach Balls

(5 dozen)

1   10-ounce package frozen chopped spinach
4   tablespoons butter
3   tablespoons minced onion
1   cup herb stuffing mix
½   cup freshly grated Parmesan cheese
Salt and freshly ground black pepper

Cook the spinach according to the package directions, drain, and squeeze out as much moisture as possible. In a small skillet melt the butter and cook the onion over low heat until soft. Do not allow it to brown. In a bowl, combine the spinach and the onion with the remaining ingredients. Allow the mixture to stand for 1 hour at room temperature.

Preheat the oven to 325°.

Shape into small balls and place on a lightly greased cookie sheet. Bake for 15 minutes. Serve hot.

Note: These balls may be frozen unbaked, but they must be fully thawed before baking.

Zucchini Squares

(6 dozen)

    2   tablespoons butter
    2   shallots, minced
    3   eggs
    ½   cup milk
    3   cups grated zucchini
    ½   cup corn oil
    ¼   teaspoon salt
Freshly ground black pepper
    1   teaspoon minced fresh parsley
    1   teaspoon minced fresh chives
    ¼   teaspoon dried oregano *or* basil
    ½   cup grated Parmesan cheese
    1   cup biscuit mix

Preheat the oven to 350°.

In a small saucepan melt the butter, add the shallots, and cook over low heat until softened. Beat the eggs in a large bowl; add the milk and all the other ingredients, including the shallots and their butter. Mix well and pour into a greased 8- by 10-inch pan. Bake for 35 minutes. When cool, cut into squares.

Note: The cooked squares may be frozen and reheated.

Soups

Sallie Y. Williams's Broccoli-Roquefort
  Soup
Morning Glory Café Chicken Soup
Sallie Y. Williams's She Crab Soup
Scallop Soup
The Chanticleer's Cold Cucumber &
  Tomato Soup
Shrimp Bisque
Cold Spinach & Basil Soup

Sallie Y. Williams's Broccoli-Roquefort Soup

(6 servings)

1 quart chicken broth, fresh *or* canned
2 cups fresh broccoli spears, cut into 2-inch lengths
1 large potato, peeled, cut in 6 pieces
1 medium onion, quartered
1 clove garlic, peeled
2–3 tablespoons Roquefort cheese
⅓ cup heavy cream

In a heavy saucepan heat the broth and add the broccoli, potato, onion, and garlic. Bring to a boil. Reduce the heat and simmer for 20 minutes or until the vegetables are tender. In a food processor, blender, or food mill purée the broccoli mixture, in batches if necessary. Return the purée to the saucepan. Add the cheese to the broccoli mixture and stir over low heat until the cheese is completely melted. Stir in the cream. Serve at once.

Note: To serve cold, chill the soup well; top each serving with a dollop of sour cream and sprinkle with chopped parsley if desired.

For faster preparation and a more nutritious soup, don't bother to peel the potato.

Morning Glory Café Chicken Soup

(10–12 servings)

2 medium baking potatoes, sliced
2 cups chopped onion
4 cloves minced garlic
3 tablespoons butter
3 tablespoons olive oil
2 teaspoons curry powder
2 cups clear chicken broth
1½ cups sour cream
Pulverized bay leaf
⅛ teaspoon Chinese 5-spice mixture
⅛ teaspoon white pepper
Sour cream (garnish)
Chopped peanuts (garnish)
Parsley or watercress sprigs (garnish)

In a skillet sauté the potatoes, onion, and garlic in the butter and oil until the potatoes are soft. Purée the vegetables in a blender or food processor, adding the curry powder. Pour into a stock pot and add the remaining ingredients (except for the garnishes). Stir to combine. Heat slowly until the soup thickens on the sides of the pot, stirring often. Do not allow it to boil. Garnish with the sour cream, peanuts, and a sprig of cress or parsley.

Note: This soup is also excellent served cold.

Sallie Y. Williams's She Crab Soup

(6 servings)

2 tablespoons butter
2 small onions, minced
2 cups crabmeat, with roe if possible
2 tablespoons flour
4 cups hot milk
Salt and freshly ground black pepper
1 teaspoon Worcestershire sauce
1 cup heavy cream
¼ cup sherry

Melt the butter in a heavy saucepan. Sauté the onions until they are transparent. Add the crabmeat and heat well. Add the flour and salt and pepper. Stir well. Add the hot milk all at once, stirring constantly but gently. Take care not to break up the crabmeat. Simmer for 10 minutes. Check the seasoning and add the Worcestershire sauce. Simmer for 10 more minutes. Add the cream and sherry and heat thoroughly, but do not boil. Serve at once.

Scallop Soup

(6–8 servings)

½ pound sea scallops, sliced
4 tablespoons butter
Sherry
3 cans vichyssoise, heated
Salt and freshly ground white pepper
Paprika

In a skillet sauté the scallops in butter until they are translucent. Add the sherry, and combine with the warm vichyssoise. Season with the salt and pepper to taste. Sprinkle with paprika. Serve in warm soup bowls.

The Chanticleer's Cold Cucumber & Tomato Soup

(6 servings)

2 pounds tomatoes, peeled, seeded, and coarsely chopped
8 cups chicken stock
3 tablespoons flour
3 tablespoons butter
1 teaspoon salt
Freshly ground black pepper
1 tablespoon sugar
Pinch of nutmeg
1 cucumber, peeled, seeded, and diced
1 tablespoon butter
1 tablespoon chopped fresh dill
1 tablespoon chopped fresh parsley
½ cup sour cream
Chopped parsley (garnish)

In a large saucepan cook the tomatoes in the chicken stock until soft. Purée a little at a time in a blender or food processor. In the same saucepan melt the 3 tablespoons butter, stir in the flour, and cook for 2 minutes. Stir in 2 cups of the tomato-chicken stock. Simmer until thickened and add the rest. Add the salt, pepper, sugar, and nutmeg, stirring until well combined, and let cool.

In a saucepan, melt the 1 tablespoon butter. Add the cucumber and stir over medium-high heat for 2 minutes, just to soften the cucumber slightly. Let cool. Add to the tomato-chicken purée. Just before serving, stir in the sour cream, dill, and parsley. Garnish with a dollop of sour cream topped with chopped parsley.

Shrimp Bisque

(10–12 servings)

2 tablespoons butter
1 small onion, grated
2 cups cooked shrimp or well-rinsed canned shrimp, finely chopped
1 quart milk
1 cup cream
Salt and freshly ground white pepper
Butter
Paprika

Melt the butter in a saucepan. Add the onion and cook for 5 minutes over low heat until it is soft but not brown. Add the shrimp and stir, then add the milk and cream. Add the salt and pepper to taste. Heat over a very low flame for 15 minutes. Serve in warmed soup bowls and top each serving with a dab of butter and paprika.

Cold Spinach & Basil Soup

(6 servings)

2 tablespoons oil
½ cup chopped onion
1½ pounds raw spinach, washed and picked over
½ cup fresh basil
3 cups chicken stock
1 cup half-and-half
½ cup plain yogurt
Salt and freshly ground black pepper
Very thin lemon slices (garnish)

In a large skillet heat the oil slightly, add the onion, and cook until soft; do not allow the onion to brown. Add the spinach and basil and cook for 1 or 2 minutes until they are wilted. Put the mixture in the bowl of a food processor or blender and add 1 cup of the chicken stock. Process until smooth. Remove the mixture to a large bowl and stir in the cream and then the yogurt. Add the remaining 2 cups of chicken stock, stir well to combine, and season with the salt and pepper to taste. Chill well. Serve garnished with the lemon slices.

Main Dishes

Main Dishes

A well-chosen main dish is the heart of any *Simple Feast*. There are dishes here to please every taste, including many meatless dishes and meatless variations of such classics as Lasagna and Stuffed Peppers. For those who favor substantial basic fare, there are delicious recipes for beef, lamb, pork, and veal — stews, ragouts, roasts, and chops.

In keeping with a now-established trend in American cuisine, many of our main dishes are made with pasta and cheese, eggs, poultry, and fish or seafood. Some can be garnished or prepared with meat (*like many of the variations on the basic Pizza recipe*), but most will stand on their own beautifully. Maurice Moore-Betty's Mushroom Soufflé is always a treat. Sallie Y. Williams's Summer Spaghetti is a primavera variation made with zucchini and fresh tomatoes; Fettuccine Alfredo is a more substantial pasta dish.

If you aren't accustomed to thinking of eggs as the main course, think again. Moderate amounts of cheese and eggs can add economy and variety to your meal planning and still fall within nutritional guidelines. Scrambled Eggs with Salmon is a rich, delicately flavored treat. Piperade and Frittata are exotic variations on the omelet theme. Cheese Soufflé is always appropriate, be it lunch or dinner, casual or carefully planned. And Cheese Fondue is a delight when it's cold outside and you are enjoying a quiet evening with friends or family.

Seafood and fish are easily adapted to many spices, herbs, and sauces. Shrimp is perhaps the most versatile of all, lending itself to salads, casseroles, and combinations with other fish or seafood and vegetables of all kinds. Joan Itoh's Boiled Shrimps and Cauliflower, with peas for color and texture, is a particularly pretty dish served in the traditional Japanese lacquered bowls.

Fish dishes are excellent main courses that can usually be prepared in little time. With a food processor to help with chopping and to blend sauces, even a dish like the Chanticleer's Fillet of Sole with Vegetables Julienne is easy to make. Scallops Marinara is another excellent dish that is simple to prepare.

Though chicken is economical and healthful, many of us find it hard to come up with new ways to serve it. Here are recipes to vary the menu in elegant and appealing ways. There are excellent recipes for turkey, too, and other poultry specialties.

Wolfgang Puck's Chicken with Tomato Fondue is simple and fast, good hot or cold, and low in calories. Richard Lavin's Tarragon Chicken is another easy, flavorful dish; try the Curry Chicken variation, made with bits of crystallized ginger, for elegance

and sliced mushrooms in a cream sauce, can be prepared ahead of time and the chicken browned at the last minute.

Chicken Livers with Onions & Artichoke Hearts may sound esoteric, but the result is delicious. And a half hour should do it — cook the rice or noodles while the dish is being prepared and is simmering to completion. Turkey Breast Tonnato is a less expensive variation of Vitello Tonnato that can be made a day early.

Beef is a long-standing American favorite, for here we raise much of the world's supply. We assume you have your own favorite way to serve roast beef, so most of our recipes are for special dishes — Chili con Carne, Beef Stew, the Russian Tea Room's Beef Stroganoff, Hungarian Goulash, Joan Itoh's Sukiyaki Donburi, and Venetian Calves' Liver.

Jean Anderson's Mushroom & Shallot Stuffed Hamburger is an example of how traditional dishes can be given new twists.

A wide variety of lamb dishes are here, including two versions of stuffed lamb (Portuguese style and Butterflied Lamb), a Réchauffé using leftovers from a roast, Souvlakia, Roast Lamb with Mustard & Ginger, and Moussaka.

Among the veal recipes, you will find a Ragout of Veal with Eggplant, Veal Scallops with Artichoke Hearts, and Jean Anderson's Wheaten Veal Chops with Lemon & Capers — all a far cry from Breaded Veal Parmesan, and all delicious. The Blanquette de Veau is a special treasure, for the simple step-by-step method enables even a beginning cook to add this excellent dish to an expanding culinary repertoire.

Eggs, Pasta & Cheese

Frittata
Linguine Primavera
Helen Corbitt's Piperade
Scrambled Eggs with Salmon
Maurice Moore-Betty's Mushroom
   Soufflé
Fettuccine Alfredo
Ziti Casserole
Sallie Y. Williams's Summer Spaghetti
Cheese Soufflé
Gougère
Pizza
Cheese Fondue
Swiss Spinach Pie
Stuffed Peppers

Frittata

(3 servings)

3 tablespoons butter
1 medium onion, chopped
½ cup chopped ham
6 eggs
¼ cup grated Parmesan cheese
Salt and freshly ground black pepper
1 small zucchini, grated coarsely

In a medium-size skillet melt 1 tablespoon of the butter and slowly cook the onion until it is golden brown. Add the ham and cook until it is browned (1–2 minutes). In a bowl beat the eggs; add the onion and ham, the cheese, and salt and pepper to taste. Wipe out the skillet, melt the remaining butter, and cook the zucchini over medium-high heat. Add the egg mixture and lower the heat. Cook until the eggs have set. Put the *frittata* under the broiler and brown until the top is golden. Cut into wedges to serve.

Note: This is an Italian omelet. You can vary the ingredients to be added to the eggs indefinitely, for many other meats, vegetables, and cheeses will work well.

Linguine Primavera

(6 servings)

1 cup broccoli florets
¼ pound snow peas, trimmed
1 cup sliced zucchini
12 asparagus spears, cut into 2-inch pieces
1 pound linguine
1 tablespoon olive oil
12 small cherry tomatoes
¼ cup fresh basil, chopped
Salt and freshly ground black pepper
4 tablespoons butter
1 cup cream
⅓ cup freshly grated Parmesan cheese
Additional grated Parmesan cheese

Cook each vegetable separately until crisp-tender. Run under cold water to stop cooking and set aside. Cook the linguine *al dente*. While the linguine is cooking, heat the oil in a skillet and sauté the tomatoes briefly. Toss them with the basil, salt and pepper to taste, and set aside. Heat the butter and cream and add the ⅓ cup Parmesan. Drain the linguine. Add the green vegetables to the cream sauce until heated through and pour the sauce over the linguine. Top with the tomatoes. Serve with more Parmesan.

Helen Corbitt's Piperade

(8 servings)

- 2 tablespoons butter
- 1 tablespoon olive oil (optional)
- 2 cloves garlic, crushed
- ½ cup thinly sliced onion
- 2 green peppers, slivered and blanched
- 4 ripe tomatoes, peeled and chopped
- 1 tablespoon plus 1 teaspoon salt
- ⅛ teaspoon white pepper
- ¼ cup chopped parsley
- 12 eggs
- Cracked pepper (garnish)
- Chopped chives *or* parsley (garnish)

In a skillet melt the butter, add the olive oil if desired, and sauté the garlic, onion, and green peppers for 1 minute. Add the tomatoes and cook slowly until all the liquid from the tomatoes has evaporated. Add the 1 tablespoon salt and the pepper and parsley. Beat the eggs lightly with the 1 teaspoon salt and stir gently into the tomato mixture. Let the eggs cook over low heat until they have set. (They should never be hard-cooked.) Slide onto a heated platter. Sprinkle with the pepper and chives or parsley.

Note: For a large group, soft-scramble the eggs and pile them on top of the tomato mixture. Eat as soon as possible in either case.

Variations: Anchovies are a nice addition for supper (not for breakfast). I use smoked sausage frequently.

Scrambled Eggs with Salmon

(2 servings)

- 5 eggs
- 2 ounces smoked salmon, chopped
- 1 tablespoon chopped fresh parsley
- ½ tablespoon dried dill
- 2 tablespoons dry white wine
- Freshly ground white pepper
- 1 tablespoon butter

Beat the eggs with all the other ingredients except the butter. Melt the butter in a medium-size skillet. Add the egg mixture to the skillet and scramble over medium heat until the eggs are soft-firm (well cooked, but not dry). Serve immediately.

Note: This is a wonderful brunch or supper dish. Accompany with crusty French bread and a cucumber salad.

Maurice Moore-Betty's Mushroom Soufflé

(6–8 servings)

- 5 tablespoons butter
- 5 tablespoons flour
- 1 teaspoon salt
- ¼ teaspoon paprika
- Dash of cayenne pepper
- 1½ cups hot milk
- ¾ cup Parmesan cheese, grated
- 6 eggs
- ½ pound mushrooms, wiped clean and sliced thin
- 2 egg whites
- Pinch of cream of tartar

In a heavy pan melt the butter and add the flour, salt, paprika, and cayenne. Cook for 3 minutes, stirring. Heat the milk to just under the boil and add it gradually to the roux (flour mixture), whisking vigorously. Add the Parmesan.

Preheat the oven to 400°.

Separate the eggs and add the yolks and the mushrooms to the sauce. Beat the 8 egg whites and the cream of tartar until stiff, then fold them into the mushroom mixture. Pour gently into a 2-quart greased soufflé dish. Mark a smaller circle on top of the soufflé with a knife so it will rise like a hat. Bake for 35 minutes.

Note: Always serve a soufflé from the center, not from the outer edge. The soufflé is fragile in the center and will hold up better if you leave the outer edges for the last servings.

Fettuccine Alfredo

(6 servings)

- 1 pound fettuccine
- 2 tablespoons salt
- ¼ pound unsalted butter
- 1 cup heavy cream, heated
- 1 cup freshly grated Parmesan cheese
- Freshly ground white pepper
- Chopped parsley (garnish)

Cook the noodles *al dente* in 4 quarts boiling water to which the salt has been added. Melt the butter in a large heatproof skillet. Drain the noodles and toss with the butter in the skillet. Add the warm cream and the cheese and stir over low heat until the cheese has melted. Season to taste with the white pepper. Sprinkle with the parsley and serve immediately on heated plates.

Variation: Add ¼ pound prosciutto, cut into julienne pieces, when the cheese has melted.

Ziti Casserole

(8 servings)

2	tablespoons olive oil
1	cup chopped onion
2	cloves garlic, minced
6	cups canned Italian plum tomatoes
2	teaspoons salt

Freshly ground black pepper

⅛	teaspoon oregano
1	teaspoon dried basil
1	pound mozzarella cheese
1	pound ricotta cheese
1½	cups cooked spinach, well drained
2	eggs, lightly beaten
½	cup Parmesan cheese
½	teaspoon salt
1	pound ziti, cooked *al dente* and drained

In a large skillet heat the olive oil and sauté the onion and garlic until golden. Add the tomatoes, the 2 teaspoons salt, pepper, oregano, and basil. Simmer for 1 hour, stirring occasionally.

Preheat the oven to 375°.

Cut one third of the mozzarella in thin slices and reserve. Cut the rest of it in small cubes and combine with the ricotta, spinach, eggs, Parmesan, and the ½ teaspoon salt in a large bowl. Spoon a little of the sauce over the bottom of a large baking pan or casserole.

Layer with half the ziti and lightly toss with two forks to distribute the filling throughout the casserole. Spoon the remaining sauce over the ziti and place the reserved mozzarella slices in a decorative pattern on top. Bake for 45 minutes.

Note: Two smaller baking pans or casseroles may be used.

Variations: Tiny meatballs or sausage slices can be added to the casserole. Cook them first, then layer them in with the other ingredients.

Sallie Y. Williams's Summer Spaghetti

(6 servings)

⅓ cup olive oil
1 large onion, finely grated
2 cloves garlic, minced
4 large tomatoes, peeled, seeded, and chopped
Salt and freshly ground black pepper
1 pound spaghetti
6 small zucchini, grated
3 tablespoons fresh basil
2 tablespoons butter
Freshly grated Parmesan cheese

Use enough olive oil to cover the bottom of a medium-size skillet. Heat well and add the onions and garlic. Reduce the heat and cook until the onion is soft and golden. Add the tomatoes and season to taste. Prepare the spaghetti *al dente* (cooked to a firm consistency). Just before it is ready, add the zucchini and basil to the tomatoes and simmer for about 5 minutes. The zucchini should be crisp. Drain the pasta well and toss with the butter. Top the spaghetti with the vegetable mixture. Serve with plenty of the grated cheese.

Cheese Soufflé

(4 servings)

Mold:
1 tablespoon butter, softened
1 tablespoon grated Gruyère cheese

Soufflé:
3 tablespoons butter
3 tablespoons flour
1 cup hot milk
½ teaspoon salt
Pinch of white pepper
4 egg yolks
6 egg whites, at room temperature
1 cup grated Gruyère cheese *or* ½ cup Gruyère and ½ cup Parmesan cheese

Preheat the oven to 400°.

To prepare the mold: Rub a 2-quart mold with the softened butter right up to the edge. Sprinkle it with the grated cheese and put aside.

To make the soufflé: In a large saucepan melt the butter and stir in the flour. Cook over medium heat, but do not allow the flour to brown. Remove from the heat and whisk in the hot milk until blended. Add the salt and pepper. Return to the heat and whisk until the sauce is smooth and thick. Let it simmer for a minute or two, then remove it from the heat. Add the egg yolks one at a time, beating after each addition to blend thoroughly. Set aside. Beat the egg whites until they are very stiff. Blend 1 large spoonful of the beaten whites into the yolk mixture to lighten it. Add the grated cheese to the yolk mixture, then fold in the egg whites carefully. Pour the mixture gently into the prepared mold and smooth the top. The dish should be three quarters full. You can make a cap on the soufflé by cutting a trench 1 inch deep, 1 inch from the edge of the mold.

Place the soufflé on the middle shelf of the oven and lower the heat to 375°. Bake for 30 to 35 minutes. Serve at once.

Gougère

(6–8 servings)

- 1 cup water
- ½ cup salted butter, cut in pieces
- ¼ teaspoon salt
- 1 cup flour
- 4 large eggs
- 5 ounces aged Gruyère cheese, grated, *or* Parmesan cheese *or* a combination of the two

Preheat the oven to 400°.

In a saucepan, bring the water to a boil with the butter and salt. When the butter has melted completely, remove the pan from the heat and add the flour all at once. Mix rapidly with a wooden spoon to blend thoroughly. Return the pan to the stove and beat the dough with a wooden spoon for 3 or 4 minutes over medium heat. The dough will leave the sides of the pan and begin to film the bottom. Remove the pan from the heat and beat in the eggs, one at a time, until the dough is shiny and thick. (This may be done in a food processor.) Beat in the cheese.

On an ungreased cookie sheet place large spoonfuls of the dough in a circle, just touching. Bake for 20 minutes; reduce the heat to 375° and bake for another 10 minutes. Serve hot. This is a lovely luncheon dish or first course.

Variations: Cut the *gougère* in half horizontally and fill with creamed fish, seafood, chicken, or lightly steamed vegetables in butter sauce.

This dough can also be made into small puffs for hors d'oeuvres. Place small spoonfuls of dough 1½ inches apart on an ungreased cookie sheet. Bake for 20 minutes at 400°. Serve warm.

Note: *Gougère* hors d'oeuvres may be frozen after forming. Thaw and bake as directed.

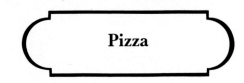

Pizza

(4–8 servings)

Tomato Sauce:
- 1 tablespoon olive oil
- 1 medium onion, chopped
- 1½ cups canned tomatoes, drained, seeded, and chopped
- ½ teaspoon oregano
- 1 bay leaf
- Salt and freshly ground black pepper

Pizza Dough:
- ½ package dried yeast
- ½ cup lukewarm water
- 2 cups all-purpose flour, sifted
- ½ teaspoon salt
- 1 tablespoon olive oil

- 1 cup shredded mozzarella cheese

To make the sauce: In a saucepan heat the oil and sauté the onion until soft but not brown. Add the remaining ingredients, bring to a boil, and simmer for ½ hour.

To make the dough: In a small bowl dissolve the yeast in the water. Sift the flour and the salt into a large bowl. Add the yeast and the oil and knead until smooth (8–10 minutes). (To mix in a food processor, process with the metal blade until a ball begins to form, then remove the dough and knead for 4 minutes.) Place the dough in a bowl, cover with a clean towel, and allow to rise in a warm place for 2 hours.

Preheat the oven to 400°.

Oil a 15-inch pizza pan. Pull and stretch the dough to fit the pan. Spread the tomato sauce over the dough and let rise another 10 minutes before cooking. Top with the mozzarella and bake for 25 minutes.

Note: To make a quick pizza: Sprinkle pita bread with olive oil, spread with canned tomato sauce, sprinkle with dried oregano and grated mozzarella or Parmesan cheese. Bake until bubbly.

Variations: Shred the mozzarella over the dough, cover with the sauce, and top with more cheese.

Slice ½ pound fresh mushrooms and sauté in 2 tablespoons of olive oil and 1 tablespoon of butter and add to the tomato sauce.

Before baking top the pizza with: finely sliced pepperoni or sliced black olives or anchovies and capers or cooked Italian sweet or hot sausage.

(Preceding Pages) Pizza & Variations

Cheese Fondue

(6 servings)

1 clove garlic, cut
1½ cups dry white wine
1¼ pounds imported Swiss cheese, cut in small pieces (use ½ Emmenthal, ½ Gruyère *or* the stronger Alpenzell)
2 tablespoons cornstarch
3 tablespoons kirsch
Freshly ground black pepper
1 long loaf French bread, cut in bite-size pieces

Rub a pottery fondue dish with the garlic. Add the wine and bring to the boiling point. Add the cheese, stirring with a wooden spoon. Mix the cornstarch with the kirsch and add it to the cheese when it has become creamy. Season with the pepper. Bring the fondue to the table and set it over a heating element. Pass a basket of French bread pieces to dip into the fondue. Serve with wooden skewers or fondue forks to hold the bread while it is being dipped into the fondue.

Note: A pottery fondue pot should be used for cheese fondues. Metal fondue pots are suitable for beef fondues.

Swiss Spinach Pie

(4–6 servings)

1 10-ounce package frozen spinach
1 medium onion, finely chopped
2 slices bacon, diced
3 eggs
1½ cups milk
1 teaspoon cornstarch
Salt and freshly ground black pepper
9- or 10-inch pie pan lined with Quick Basic Pie Crust

Preheat the oven to 400°.

Thaw the spinach and press out all the water. In a small skillet sauté the onions with the bacon until brown. Beat the eggs. In a saucepan heat the milk with the cornstarch and add to the eggs. Return the eggs to the pan and stir over low heat until thickened. Combine the eggs with the spinach, bacon, and onions and season with the salt and pepper. Pour into the pastry shell and bake for 40 minutes.

Stuffed Peppers

(6 servings)

6   green or red peppers, seeded and
    cored
2   tablespoons olive oil
1   cup chopped onion
1   cup chopped mushrooms
3   cups cooked rice
½   cup pitted black olives (optional)
2   tablespoons chopped parsley
1   teaspoon dried basil
Salt and freshly ground black pepper
2   cups tomato juice

Preheat the oven to 350°.

Place the peppers in a baking pan that allows them to fit tightly.

In a large skillet heat the oil and sauté the onion until it has wilted. Add the mushrooms and cook until they are soft. Add the rice, olives, parsley, basil, and salt and pepper and mix. Taste for seasonings and adjust. Add enough tomato juice to moisten the mixture. Stuff the peppers with the mixture and pour the rest of the tomato juice over and around them. Bake for 45 to 60 minutes, until the peppers are tender.

Note: This stuffing can also be used for tomatoes. Adjust the cooking time accordingly (tomatoes will cook much faster).

Variation: Substitute any leftover cooked meat, fish, or poultry for 1 cup of the cooked rice.

Fish & Seafood

Paella
Maurice Moore-Betty's Seafood
  Fricassee
Cold Pasta & Seafood Salad
Baked Scallops
Scallops Marinara
Scallops & Shrimp Velouté
Hot Salmon Mousse
Elizabeth Esterling's Salmon Loaf
Bluefish S'conset
Stir-fried Shrimp & Vegetables
Mary's Shrimp & Rice Casserole
Shrimp-stuffed Crown Artichokes
Shrimp & Artichoke Hearts

Joan Itoh's Boiled Shrimps &
  Cauliflower
Zucchini Maison with Shrimp
Parmesan Fish Fillets
Crunchy Fish Fillets
The Chanticleer's Fillet of Sole with
  Chives
Fillet of Sole with Mushrooms
Fillet of Sole Florentine
The Chanticleer's Fillet of Sole with
  Vegetables Julienne
Broiled Swordfish with Béarnaise
  Sauce

Paella

(6 servings)

- 6 small Spanish or Italian sausages
- 6 tablespoons olive oil
- 1 3-pound chicken, cut into small serving pieces
- ¾ cup chopped onions
- 1 clove garlic, minced
- ½ cup chopped sweet red pepper
- 1 cup raw rice
- 1 1-pound can tomatoes, drained and chopped
- 2 cups chicken stock or broth heated with ⅛ teaspoon saffron powder

Salt and freshly ground black pepper
- 1 pound shrimp, peeled and deveined
- 1½ dozen small littleneck clams *or* mussels, well scrubbed
- 1 package frozen peas

Place the sausage in a small saucepan, cover with water, and bring to a boil. Simmer for 20 minutes, then prick the sausage to release the fat. Remove the sausage from the pan and drain on paper towels. Heat the olive oil in a large heatproof casserole and brown the chicken pieces on all sides. Remove them from the pot and reserve. Cut the sausage in 1-inch lengths and brown them in the casserole. Remove them from the pot and reserve. Pour off all but 2 tablespoons of oil from the casserole and cook the onions in the oil until they are golden. Add the garlic and red pepper and cook over low heat for 3 minutes. (Do not allow the garlic to brown, or it will become bitter.) Stir in the rice and cook for a few minutes, until the rice becomes opaque. Stir in the tomatoes, saffron chicken stock or broth, and salt and pepper. Bring to a boil, cover the casserole tightly, and reduce the heat to a simmer. Cook for 20 minutes.

Preheat the oven to 325°.

Remove the casserole from heat, fluff the rice, add the chicken and sausage, and stir gently. Cover the casserole and bake for 10 minutes. Add the shrimp and the peas and stir gently. Add the clams or mussels in their shells and return to the oven, covered, for 10 more minutes.

Before serving, discard any clams or mussels that have not opened. The paella may be served from the casserole or on a large platter.

Maurice Moore-Betty's Seafood Fricassee

(6 servings)

- ½ pound small fresh shrimp, peeled and deveined
- ½ pound fresh-frozen lobster, thawed and drained
- ½ pound fresh-frozen crabmeat, thawed and drained
- ½ pound bay scallops
- 2 ounces (½ stick) butter
- ½ cup tomato purée
- ½ cup dry white vermouth
- ½ pound mushrooms, sliced thin
- 2 tablespoons cornstarch
- ½ cup heavy cream
- Salt and freshly ground black pepper
- ½ cup parsley sprigs, chopped (garnish)

Wash the shrimp and cut them in half lengthwise. Rinse the lobster, crabmeat, and scallops under cold running water.

Melt the butter in a heavy pan or skillet. Add the shrimp and cook, turning with a spoon, for 3 to 4 minutes. Add the scallops and cook for 3 minutes longer. Stir in the tomato purée and add the vermouth. Add the lobster, mushrooms, and crabmeat and cook 2 minutes longer.

Moisten the cornstarch with a little water to make a smooth paste, mix with the cream, and stir into the seafood mixture. Season with salt and pepper to taste and heat until thickened. Serve sprinkled with the chopped parsley.

Note: If fresh lobster and crabmeat are available, use them.

Cold Pasta & Seafood Salad

(4–6 servings)

- 1 pound fettuccine or linguine, cooked *al dente*
- ½ pound cooked seafood: lobster, shrimp, crabmeat, any firm-fleshed white fish *or* any combination
- ¼ pound mushrooms, sliced and sautéed lightly in butter
- 1 cup cooked peas
- 1 tablespoon chopped fresh chives
- 4 tablespoons diced red pepper or pimiento
- ½ cup Vinaigrette (more if you prefer)

Combine all the ingredients and toss. Serve with sliced tomato sprinkled with chopped fresh basil, garlic bread, and chilled white wine.

Baked Scallops

(4 servings)

- 1 tablespoon butter
- ¾ pound mushrooms, sliced
- 2 tablespoons melted butter
- 1 pound bay scallops *or* 1 pound sea scallops, quartered
- ½ cup heavy cream
- Salt and freshly ground white pepper
- ½ cup bread crumbs

Preheat the oven to 375°.

In a skillet melt the butter and sauté the mushroom slices. Place a little of the melted butter in each scallop shell or individual baking dish, then add the scallops and mushrooms. Reserve the remaining melted butter. Spoon the cream over the scallops and mushrooms and season with the salt and pepper. Sprinkle with the crumbs and the reserved melted butter. Bake for 10 minutes.

Scallops Marinara

(4 servings)

- 3 tablespoons olive oil
- 1 medium onion, chopped
- ½ pound mushrooms, sliced
- 1 clove garlic, crushed
- 1 28-ounce can Italian plum tomatoes
- ¾ cup dry white wine
- 3 tablespoons tomato paste
- 2 tablespoons chopped parsley
- 1 teaspoon dried oregano
- 1 tablespoon dried basil
- Salt and freshly ground black pepper
- 1½ pounds sea scallops

In a large saucepan heat the oil and cook the onion until it is wilted. Add the mushrooms and garlic. Cook for 2 minutes, then add all the other ingredients except the scallops. Bring to a boil. Reduce the heat and simmer for 1 hour. Taste and adjust the seasonings if necessary. Add the scallops to the sauce and cook for 3 or 4 minutes. Serve with rice or spaghetti.

Scallops & Shrimp Velouté

(6 servings)

    2 cups white wine
    1 cup water
    1 carrot, chopped
    1 onion, chopped
    2 sprigs parsley
    Salt and freshly ground black pepper
    6 ounces shrimp, peeled and deveined
    2 pounds bay scallops

Velouté Sauce:
    2 tablespoons butter
    2 tablespoons flour
    ½ cup milk
    ½ cup wine
    1 cup cooking liquid
    ½ cup Parmesan cheese (optional)

In a large saucepan combine the wine, water, carrot, onion, parsley, salt, and pepper and cook for 15 minutes. Cook the shrimp and scallops separately in the liquid just until firm. Do not overcook. Set the seafood aside. Boil the liquid until it has been reduced by half.

To make the sauce: In a skillet melt the butter, add the flour, and cook for 1 minute. Remove from the heat and add the milk and wine. Return to the heat and stir constantly until the sauce has thickened. Add the liquid in which the seafood was cooked and cook for 5 minutes more. Add the cheese. Return scallops and shrimp to the sauce and heat through. Serve with rice.

Hot Salmon Mousse

(6–8 servings)

    1½ pounds salmon
    2   egg whites, stiffly beaten
    2   cups heavy cream
    2   tablespoons chopped parsley
    Salt and freshly ground white pepper

Preheat the oven to 350°.

Using the food processor or meat grinder, purée the raw salmon. Fold in the egg whites and then the cream, parsley, and seasonings to taste. Oil a 4-cup mold and fill it with the fish mixture. Place the mold in a rectangular cake pan filled three quarters full with hot water. Bake for 30 minutes. Serve with Hollandaise sauce.

Elizabeth Esterling's Salmon Loaf

(6 servings)

  1 tablespoon chopped onion
  3 eggs, separated
  ½ teaspoon salt
  ½ teaspoon paprika
  3 tablespoons softened butter
  ½ cup tomato juice
  2 7-ounce cans salmon
  ½ cup dry bread crumbs

Preheat the oven to 325° and butter a loaf pan.

In a bowl mix the onion, egg yolks, salt, paprika, butter, and tomato juice. Remove the skin from the salmon and add the salmon and bread crumbs to the onion mixture. Beat the egg whites and fold into the salmon mixture. Pour the mixture into the loaf pan and bake for 1 to 1¼ hours, until lightly browned. Serve hot with Lemon Sauce or cold with Cucumber Sauce.

Bluefish S'conset

(6 servings)

  2 pounds bluefish fillets
  ¾ cup sour cream
  2 tablespoons Dijon mustard, or to taste
  2 teaspoons dried dill *or* 1 teaspoon dried thyme
Salt and freshly ground black pepper
Paprika

Preheat the oven to 375°.

Place the bluefish, skin side down, in a foil-lined baking pan. In a mixing bowl combine the sour cream, mustard, and herbs and spread it over the fish in a thick layer. Season with the salt, pepper, and paprika. Bake until the fish flakes when poked with the tip of a knife (15–20 minutes).

Note: The cream and mustard in this recipe kill the oiliness of the fish, making it a very pleasant dish. You may also remove the dark meat before cooking if you wish, as it contains the oil.

Variation: For a lower-calorie dish, substitute yogurt for the sour cream.

Stir-fried Shrimp & Vegetables

(3 servings)

- 3 tablespoons soy sauce
- 2 tablespoons dry sherry
- 2 teaspoons minced fresh ginger
- 1 clove garlic, minced
- 1 pound raw shrimp, shelled and deveined
- 1 cup broccoli florets
- 4 tablespoons vegetable oil
- 1 sweet red pepper, cut in julienne pieces
- ½ pound snow peas, trimmed
- ¾ cup sliced water chestnuts

In a bowl or shallow pan make a marinade of the soy, sherry, ginger, and garlic. Marinate the shrimp for 20 minutes. Bring a quart of salted water to a boil. Add the broccoli, bring to a second boil, and cook for 4 minutes. Drain the broccoli in a colander, refresh it at once under cold running water, and set aside.

Heat the oil in a wok or a deep skillet. Add the red pepper, stirring constantly, then the broccoli, then the shrimp, while continuing to stir. When the shrimp begins to turn white, add the snow peas and the water chestnuts. Add the marinade and bring it quickly to a boil. Simmer until the shrimp are just cooked, about 3 minutes. Serve immediately with rice.

Mary's Shrimp & Rice Casserole

(4 servings)

- 1 cup shrimp, peeled, deveined, and lightly cooked
- 2 cups cooked rice
- 6 tablespoons ketchup
- ½ teaspoon Worcestershire sauce
- ¼ teaspoon Tabasco sauce
- 1 pint light cream
- Salt to taste

Preheat the oven to 350°. Butter a 1-quart casserole.

In a bowl combine all the ingredients and place the mixture in the buttered casserole. Heat until bubbly. Serve with herb bread and a salad of green beans and mushrooms.

Note: This recipe can be increased to please a crowd.

Shrimp-stuffed Crown Artichokes

(4 servings)

- 4 artichokes of equal size bottoms and tips of leaves trimmed
- Salt
- 1 tablespoon fresh lemon juice
- 24 medium-sized shrimp, cooked, peeled, and deveined
- Hollandaise sauce

Place the artichokes in boiling water to which the salt and lemon juice have been added. Boil them until the leaves can be removed easily, about 40 minutes. Let the artichokes cool. Scoop out the center of each artichoke with a spoon or melon baller, removing the choke. The bottom should be visible. Place a little Hollandaise sauce in each artichoke cavity, and top with the shrimp, 6 shrimp to a portion. Serve at room temperature.

Note: This would make a good luncheon dish or hearty first course.

Variations: Mayonnaise with mustard or Vinaigrette may be substituted for the Hollandaise.

Shrimp & Artichoke Hearts

(6 servings)

- 1 package frozen artichoke hearts
- 1 egg yolk
- ¼ cup peanut oil
- ¼ cup olive oil
- 1 tablespoon vinegar
- 1 teaspoon Dijon mustard
- 2 tablespoons minced parsley
- 2 tablespoons minced chives
- Salt and freshly ground black pepper
- 48 medium-size shrimp, cooked

Cook the artichoke hearts according to the package directions, drain, and chill. In a bowl beat together the egg yolk, oils, vinegar, and the mustard. Add the parsley and chives and season to taste with the salt and pepper. Marinate the shrimp and artichoke hearts in this mixture for at least 2 hours. Serve as an entrée in the summer or on small plates as an appetizer year-round.

Joan Itoh's Boiled Shrimps & Cauliflower

(2 servings)

4   tablespoons *shoyu*
4   tablespoons water
2½   tablespoons *mirin*
12   large shrimp, peeled and deveined
1   small cauliflower, divided into florets
6   ounces shelled peas

In a saucepan bring the *shoyu*, water, and *mirin* to a boil. Add the shrimp and boil until they are pink. Remove the shrimp with a slotted spoon and keep hot. Cook the cauliflower until just tender in the liquid left over from the shrimps. Add the peas and cook just until tender. Serve the shrimp, cauliflower, and peas together in small bowls, allowing 6 shrimp per person.

Zucchini Maison with Shrimp

(4 servings)

4 large zucchini (about 2 pounds)
1 shallot, minced
2 tablespoons butter
4 tomatoes, peeled, seeded, and chopped
1 teaspoon paprika
Salt and freshly ground black pepper
3 ounces cooked shrimp, chopped
1 recipe Mornay Sauce
1 tablespoon grated Gruyère cheese

Preheat the oven to 400°.

Blanch the zucchini in boiling water for 6 minutes, drain, and reserve. Sauté the shallot in the butter until it is soft. Add the tomatoes, paprika, and the salt and pepper to the shallot. Halve the zucchini lengthwise, scoop out the inside flesh, and add it to the tomato mixture. Cook the mixture briefly over high heat to reduce the liquid. Add the shrimp and fill the zucchini halves with the mixture. Place the stuffed zucchini halves in a baking dish. Cover with the Mornay Sauce, sprinkle with the cheese, and bake for 20 minutes or until golden brown.

Vegetarian Variations: Substitute ½ cup herb stuffing mix or cooked rice for the shrimp.

Parmesan Fish Fillets

(6 servings)

½ cup Parmesan cheese
½ cup finely minced onion
⅓ cup Mayonnaise
6 small or 3 large fillets (sole, flounder, scrod, *or* any other thin whitefish)
Salt and freshly ground black pepper
Paprika

Make a paste of the Parmesan, onion, and mayonnaise and spread it on the fillets. Season with the salt, pepper, and paprika. Broil or bake at 375° until brown (10 to 15 minutes, depending on the size of the fillets).

Crunchy Fish Fillets

(4 servings)

4 fillets of sole *or* flounder
1 cup herb stuffing mix (grated, not cubed)
2 tablespoons vermouth or white wine
2 tablespoons butter
Chopped parsley (garnish)

Preheat the oven to 350°.

Grease a flat baking pan and lay the fillets in it. Cover the fish with the stuffing mix, sprinkle with the vermouth, and dot with the butter. Bake for about 15 minutes. Sprinkle with the parsley and serve.

The Chanticleer's Fillet of Sole with Chives

(4 servings)

4 medium-sized fillets of sole (about 1 pound)
Salt and freshly ground black pepper
½ cup (1 stick) butter, clarified
4 tablespoons bread crumbs
¾ cup fish stock *or* bottled clam juice
¼ cup vermouth
¼ cup white wine
1 tablespoon minced shallots, cooked until soft in 2 teaspoons butter
½ cup heavy cream
1 teaspoon tomato paste
1 tablespoon lemon juice
1 tablespoon butter
4 teaspoons chopped chives

Preheat the oven to 375°.

Season the sole with the salt and pepper. Roll it in the clarified butter and dredge one side in the bread crumbs. Place the fish in a buttered pan (just large enough to hold it) with ½ cup of the fish stock. Pour the rest of the butter over the bread crumbs and bake for about 8 minutes (if necessary, brown the bread crumbs under the broiler). Remove the fish to a warm plate or platter. To the pan juices add the vermouth, wine, the rest of the fish stock, and the shallots. Bring to a boil and reduce by half. Add the cream and tomato paste; reduce again until thick. Add the lemon juice and stir in the 1 tablespoon butter. Spoon the sauce over the fish and sprinkle with the chives.

Note: To clarify butter: Melt the butter in a small pan over low heat. Remove from the heat and allow the solids to sink to the bottom. The clear portion is clarified. It is far less apt to burn when heated.

Fillet of Sole with Mushrooms

(4 servings)

6 tablespoons butter
6 large mushrooms, chopped fine
2 shallots, minced
2 tablespoons minced parsley
4 fillets of sole *or* flounder
¾ cup white wine
Salt and freshly ground white pepper

Preheat the oven to 350°.

In a small baking dish melt 4 tablespoons of the butter and add the mushrooms, shallots, 1 tablespoon of the parsley, the wine, and salt and pepper. Bake for 10 minutes. Remove half of the mixture and set aside. Place the fillets on top of the mixture in the baking dish. Cover with the reserved mixture and dot with 1 tablespoon of the remaining butter. Bake for 15 more minutes. Remove the fish to hot plates and keep warm. In a saucepan over medium heat reduce the sauce and swirl in the remaining tablespoon of butter. Pour the sauce over the fish and sprinkle with the remaining minced parsley.

Fillet of Sole Florentine

(6 servings)

4 tablespoons butter
Salt and freshly ground black pepper
Nutmeg
2 packages frozen chopped spinach
¼ pound fresh mushrooms
½ cup heavy cream
6 fillets of sole *or* flounder
Mornay Sauce

In a saucepan combine ¼ cup water, 2 tablespoons of the butter, and the salt, pepper, and nutmeg. Allow the spinach to defrost partially and cut it into small cubes so it will cook evenly. Add the spinach to the saucepan. Cover and cook until the spinach is completely thawed. Remove the cover and cook over medium heat for 5 to 10 minutes, until the spinach is tender and most of the water has evaporated. Squeeze out all liquid from the spinach and set aside.

Slice the mushrooms and cook in a skillet with the remaining butter until they are soft but not brown. Add the cream and bring to a boil, stirring constantly. Stir in the reserved spinach. Taste and add salt and pepper if needed.

Preheat the oven to 375° and butter a baking dish.

Spread the spinach mixture in the baking dish. Fold the sole fillets in half and place them on top of the spinach. Cover with the Mornay sauce and bake for 10 to 12 minutes.

Note: This dish may be prepared ahead of time. After placing the fillets on the spinach mixture, cover the baking dish and refrigerate it. A half hour before you are ready to serve, preheat the oven, cover the fillets with the Mornay sauce, bake, and serve immediately.

The Chanticleer's Fillet of Sole with Vegetables Julienne

(4 servings)

1 lime
1 carrot
1 stalk celery
1 leek, white part only
2 shallots, chopped
4 tablespoons butter
Salt and freshly ground black pepper
1 pound fillet of sole
2 tablespoons chopped parsley
¼ cup flour
¾ cup white wine
¾ cup heavy cream
Chopped parsley (garnish)

Peel the zest from the lime. Squeeze the lime and reserve the juice. Cut the vegetables and the lime zest into julienne pieces. Melt 2 tablespoons of the butter in a skillet and cook the lime zest and the vegetables over medium heat until tender. Season with the salt and pepper. Marinate the fish in the lime juice, additional salt and pepper, and chopped parsley for 30 minutes.

Lightly flour the fish and sauté it in the remaining butter until it is lightly browned. Remove the fish to a hot plate. Deglaze the pan with the wine. Reduce the heat and add the cream, the vegetables, and the lime zest. Season to taste. Pour the sauce over the fish and garnish with more chopped parsley.

Broiled Swordfish with Béarnaise Sauce

(6–8 servings)

4 tablespoons butter, melted
1 bay leaf
2 tablespoons lemon juice
3 pounds swordfish, cut 1 inch thick
Salt and freshly ground black pepper
1 recipe Béarnaise Sauce

Preheat the broiler.

In a small saucepan melt the butter with the bay leaf and add the lemon juice. Using a pastry brush, coat both sides of the fish with the seasoned butter, then place the fish on the broiler pan. Season with the salt and pepper. Place the pan about 3 inches from the heat and cook for 3 minutes. Brush the fish again with the butter and cook for 5 more minutes. Turn the fish, brush again, and cook for 3 more minutes. Butter once more and cook 5 minutes. (The total cooking time is about 15 minutes.) The broiled fish should be brown and firm. Serve immediately. Pass the Béarnaise in a warm sauceboat.

Poultry

Wolfgang Puck's Chicken with
    Tomato Fondue
Broiled Orange Chicken
Honeyed Chicken
Richard Lavin's Tarragon Chicken
Chicken Mornay
Chicken Kebabs
Barbecued Chicken
Helen Witty's Chicken Scallops in
    Paprika Cream
Chicken Hash
Coq au Vin
Chicken Pojarski
Gloria Pepin's Chicken with Rice
    (*Arroz con Pollo*)

Joan Itoh's Stuffed Pumpkin Japanese
Chicken Cutlets in Cream
Island Chicken
Chicken Cacciatore
Exotic Chicken Salad
Chicken or Turkey Tetrazzini
Turkey Breast Tonnato
Maurice Moore-Betty's Turkey
    Scallopine with Marsala
Game Hens with Cherries
Chicken Livers with Onions &
    Artichoke Hearts

Wolfgang Puck's Chicken with Tomato Fondue

(4 servings)

½ large onion, sliced
½ tablespoon olive oil
1 medium bell pepper, cut in 1-inch cubes
1 medium zucchini, cut in 1-inch cubes
6 tomatoes, peeled, seeded, and quartered
1 3½-pound chicken, cut in 8 pieces
Pinch of thyme
2 cloves garlic, chopped
1 teaspoon salt
½ teaspoon freshly ground pepper

In a skillet over medium heat, sauté the onion in the olive oil until it is translucent. Add the bell pepper and zucchini and sauté 5 minutes longer. Add the tomatoes and cook until the vegetables are tender.

Sauté the chicken pieces in a nonstick skillet until they are golden brown. Drain the grease from the skillet.

Preheat the oven to 375°.

Place half the vegetables in the bottom of a 1½-quart casserole. Arrange the chicken over the vegetables and top with the remaining vegetables. Season with the thyme, garlic, salt, and pepper. Cover and bake for 30 minutes. Serve from the casserole, either hot or cold.

Note: A good example of *cuisine minceur,* this dish is low in calories and high in flavor.

Broiled Orange Chicken

(4 servings)

1 3-pound chicken, cleaned and quartered
2 tablespoons butter, melted
½ cup orange juice
½ cup vermouth
Salt and freshly ground black pepper

Broil the chicken, skin side down, for 5 minutes. Turn and brush with the butter. Continue to broil until it is a pale gold. Remove from broiler and lower the heat to 375°.

Pour the orange juice and vermouth over the chicken. Season with the salt and pepper. Cover the pan with foil and bake the chicken for 20 minutes. Turn the chicken and baste it, raise the heat, and return the pan to the broiler for 10 more minutes or until the chicken is brown.

Honeyed Chicken

(4 servings)

Stock for Sauce:

Chicken giblets (without the liver)
2 cups cold water
1 carrot
1 onion
3 parsley stems
Salt and freshly ground black pepper

Stuffing:

1 small onion, chopped
2 tablespoons butter, melted
½ cup ground walnuts
Fresh bread crumbs made from 3 slices
    of white bread
Zest of 1 lemon
1 tablespoon chopped parsley
½ teaspoon ground cinnamon
1 teaspoon ground sage
1 teaspoon thyme
Salt and freshly ground black pepper
1 egg

1 4- to 5-pound roasting chicken, rinsed
    and dried
1 tablespoon butter, softened
2 tablespoons honey
Juice of ½ lemon
1 tablespoon arrowroot dissolved in a
    little cold water

In a saucepan combine the ingredients for the stock and place the pan over medium-low heat.

In a skillet sauté the onion in 1 tablespoon of the butter until it is transparent. Sauté the nuts separately in the remaining tablespoon of butter. Combine the rest of the stuffing ingredients in a bowl and add the cooked onions and nuts.

Preheat the oven to 350°.

Stuff the chicken, close the cavity, and place the chicken in a small roasting pan. Spread the softened butter over the chicken and roast it for 1 hour. Spread the honey over the chicken and roast for an additional 45 minutes. Remove the chicken to a serving platter and keep warm. Pour the fat from the pan, deglaze the pan with the stock and lemon juice, and strain the gravy into a saucepan. Add the arrowroot paste and cook the gravy for 2 or 3 minutes to thicken. Adjust the seasoning if necessary with salt and pepper. Serve the chicken and pass the gravy in a warm sauceboat.

Richard Lavin's Tarragon Chicken

(4 servings)

4 boneless chicken breasts, skin removed, cleaned of all fat and gristle
Water *or* chicken stock
2 bay leaves
1 teaspoon thyme
1 teaspoon whole black peppercorns
½ cup Mayonnaise, preferably homemade
3 teaspoons minced stemless fresh tarragon leaves
Blanched string beans (garnish)
Tomato wedges or slices (garnish)

Preheat the oven to 350°.

Place the chicken breasts in a shallow baking pan, cover with the water or stock, and add the bay leaves, thyme, and peppercorns. Poach in the oven, uncovered, for 35 minutes. Remove the chicken breasts from the oven and rinse immediately under cold water to prevent further cooking. Cut the chicken lengthwise into julienne strips. In a bowl place the chicken strips, mayonnaise, and tarragon and toss. Serve chilled, garnished with cold string beans and tomatoes.

Curry Chicken: Whisk together 1½ teaspoons of curry powder and ½ cup Vinaigrette and toss with the julienne of poached chicken.

Serve chilled, over a bed of red cabbage, and garnish with pieces of crystallized ginger.

Chicken Mornay

(4 servings)

4 chicken breasts, boned
3 tablespoons butter
¼ pound mushrooms, sliced
2 tablespoons flour
1 cup milk
¼ pound Gruyère cheese, freshly grated
Salt and freshly ground black pepper

In a skillet sauté the chicken in 1 tablespoon of the butter for 10 minutes. Remove the chicken to an ovenproof dish. Sauté the mushrooms in the same skillet, remove, and place on top of the chicken. Melt the remaining butter in the skillet and stir in the flour. Cook for 1 minute and stir in the milk. Cook the sauce for 5 minutes and remove from the heat. Stir in the cheese and add the salt and pepper to taste. Pour the sauce over the chicken. Brown under the broiler and serve immediately.

Note: This dish can be prepared ahead of time, but the chicken should be browned just before you are ready to serve.

Chicken Kebabs

(4–6 servings)

    2 whole chicken breasts, split, boned,
      and skinned
    2 red bell peppers
    2 navel oranges
    1 8-ounce can pineapple chunks

Marinade:
    ½ cup vegetable oil
    ½ cup white wine
    ¼ cup soy sauce
    1 tablespoon minced fresh ginger

Cut each chicken breast lengthwise into 3 pieces. Cut the peppers into pieces approximately 2 inches square. Blanch the pepper pieces by dropping them into boiling water and cooking for 1½ minutes. Refresh them under cold running water so they will stop cooking and retain their color. In a large bowl combine the marinade ingredients. Add the chicken, fruits, and the pepper, toss and let marinate for 30 minutes. Thread the different pieces onto skewers and broil or barbecue until just done, not more than 5 minutes to a side.

Barbecued Chicken

(6 servings)

    2 frying chickens, quartered
    1 recipe Barbecue Sauce *or* 1 18-ounce
      bottle commercial barbecue sauce
    1 8-ounce can tomato sauce
    Juice of ½ lemon

Preheat the oven to 350°.

Place the chicken, skin side up, in a roasting pan and bake for 20 minutes. Combine the sauces and the lemon juice in a saucepan and bring to a boil. Cook the chicken over charcoal, turning it frequently and painting it with the sauce, until it is brown and crunchy, approximately 20 minutes. Or turn up the oven to 400° and cook for 20 minutes, basting and turning frequently.

Helen Witty's Chicken Scallops in Paprika Cream

(4 servings)

2 whole chicken breasts, boned
  and skinned
Salt
Flour
2 tablespoons oil
2 tablespoons butter
1 clove garlic, flattened (or more to
  taste)
2 scallions, trimmed and sliced,
  including the green tops
2 teaspoons mild *or* medium-hot paprika
  (or more to taste)
1 cup heavy cream
Minced parsley *or* snipped chives
  (garnish)

Slice the breasts into scallops (easier if the meat is slightly frozen first). Cut across the grain on the bias, holding the knife almost flat, into slices about ½ inch thick. Lay the pieces between sheets of waxed paper and pound lightly until they are half their original thickness. Sprinkle with the salt and dust lightly with the flour.

Heat the oil and butter in a skillet. When the foam of the butter dies down, add the garlic, then the scallops, and sauté them over medium heat until just golden on both sides, 3 to 4 minutes in all. Remove and keep warm. Discard the garlic.

Pour off any excess fat from the pan and stir the scallions in the remaining fat for a moment over medium heat. Add the paprika and blend. Stir in the cream and simmer for 1 to 2 minutes, until it thickens slightly. Return the scallops to the sauce and reheat briefly. Garnish with minced parsley or snipped chives.

Chicken Hash

(4 servings)

2 cups cooked chicken, chopped
1 cup cream
2 tablespoons butter
2 tablespoons flour
1 cup milk
Salt and freshly ground white pepper

In a saucepan cook the chicken in the cream over a medium-low flame until it is heated through. Make a white sauce with the remaining ingredients and add to the chicken. Cook for a few minutes, taste for seasonings, and adjust if necessary. Place the chicken mixture in a greased flat baking dish and brown it quickly under the broiler. Serve with a green vegetable.

Coq au Vin

(4 servings)

¼ pound salt pork *or* lean bacon, dried
1 4-pound chicken, cut into serving pieces
½ cup brandy
2 tablespoons butter
10 small white onions, peeled
½ pound small mushrooms, or large ones quartered
2 tablespoons flour
1½ cups red wine
Bouquet garni: parsley stems, thyme, and a bay leaf tied in cheesecloth
Freshly ground black pepper

In a large skillet or heavy casserole cook the salt pork until it is brown and drain it on paper towels. Brown the chicken pieces on all sides. Warm the brandy, ignite, and pour over the chicken. Remove the chicken from the pan, add the butter, and brown the onions, then the mushrooms. Stir in the flour and cook for 1 minute. Add the red wine and stir until slightly thickened. Return the chicken to the pan. Add the bouquet garni and pepper to taste. Cover and simmer for 45 minutes.

Variation: Add some parboiled pieces of potato after the chicken has simmered for 30 minutes.

Chicken Pojarski

(8 servings)

1 cup fresh white bread crumbs
½ cup milk
2 pounds chicken breasts, ground
1 egg, slightly beaten
½ cup heavy cream
3 tablespoons butter, softened
Salt and freshly ground white pepper
Nutmeg
1½ cups dry bread crumbs, finely ground
6 tablespoons butter

Soak the fresh bread crumbs in the milk and squeeze out. Combine them with the ground chicken, egg, cream, softened butter, and seasonings and mix well. Form the mixture into 8 patties. Coat the patties with the dry bread crumbs and chill for at least 1 hour. Sauté in the butter until golden, about 5 minutes on each side.

Note: A food processor is perfect for this recipe.

Gloria Pepin's Chicken with Rice (Arroz con Pollo)

(4–6 servings)

- 1   3-pound chicken, cut into 8 pieces, plus 2 extra legs with thighs, cut in half
- 2   teaspoons salt
- 1¼ teaspoons pepper
- ¼ cup vegetable oil
- 2   medium onions, coarsely chopped
- 1   4½-ounce jar *alcaparrado* (olive, caper, pimiento mixture)
- ½ teaspoon oregano
- ¼ teaspoon rosemary
- ¼ teaspoon sage
- ⅛ teaspoon ground cumin
- 2   cups converted rice
- 1   large garlic clove, minced

Sprinkle the chicken with 1 teaspoon of the salt and 1 teaspoon of the pepper. Heat the oil in a large skillet that has a cover. Add the chicken, skin side down, and cook over moderate heat for about 5 minutes, or until the chicken is nicely browned. Turn the chicken and add the onions, stirring to coat them with the oil. Cook for another 5 minutes, or until the chicken is brown and the onions are translucent.

Pour the *alcaparrado* into a sieve and rinse under cold running water to wash off the brine. Add to the chicken. Sprinkle on the oregano, rosemary, sage, and cumin. Pour the rice over the chicken and stir to coat with the oil.

Add 4 cups hot tap water, stirring to make sure the rice is submerged in the liquid. Add the garlic and the remaining salt and pepper. Bring the liquid to a boil. Cover, reduce the heat, and simmer for 20 minutes. Remove from the heat. Check the seasoning, adding additional salt and pepper if needed. Allow the dish to stand, covered, for an additional 15 minutes before serving.

Joan Itoh's Stuffed Pumpkin Japanese

(4 servings)

- 1 small pumpkin, about 2 pounds
- Salt
- 1 block tofu, about 10 ounces
- 3 dried mushrooms
- 2 teaspoons sugar
- 1 carrot, diced
- 8 ounces raw chicken, minced
- 1 cup chicken stock
- 1 teaspoon cornstarch
- 1 tablespoon cold water

Cut off the top of the pumpkin. The pumpkin serves both as the main vegetable and as the cooking pot for this dish.

Remove the pumpkin seeds and sprinkle the inside of the pumpkin with salt. Put the tofu in a muslin bag and squeeze out the surplus moisture. Soak the mushrooms in water to soften, remove the stems, and cut the caps into strips. Mash the tofu thoroughly to eliminate any lumps, add ½ teaspoon salt, the sugar, carrot, mushrooms, and chicken; mix well. Stuff the pumpkin with the mixture and steam until tender (40 minutes to 1 hour). Season the stock with salt and heat. Dilute the cornstarch with the water and blend into the hot stock. Cook until the sauce thickens, stirring constantly. Pour the sauce over the stuffed pumpkin and serve.

Note: Tofu, a curd made from the soybean, comes in a great many forms and shapes. Plain tofu looks like a small white block of well-formed custard and is usually packed in about 10-ounce portions.

Variation: Chopped prawns and peas may be substituted for the chicken and carrots.

Chicken Cutlets in Cream

(8 servings)

- 4 whole chicken breasts, skinned and boned
- 4 tablespoons butter
- 2 tablespoons brandy
- ½ pound mushrooms, sliced
- 4 tablespoons flour
- 1 cup chicken stock
- 1 cup cream

Salt and freshly ground white pepper

In a large skillet lightly brown the chicken breasts in the butter. Heat the brandy, ignite, and pour over the chicken. Remove the chicken from the pan, add the mushrooms, and cook for 5 minutes. Remove the pan from the heat and add the flour. Return to the heat and cook the flour for 2 minutes, stirring constantly so it does not brown. Add the stock and stir until the mixture boils and thickens. Add the cream and salt and pepper to taste. Stir until the sauce is smooth and return the chicken to the pan. Cover and cook for another 15 to 20 minutes.

Island Chicken

(6 servings)

- 2 cucumbers, thinly sliced
- 3 whole chicken breasts, split and boned
- 2 tablespoons butter
- 2 tablespoons vermouth
- Salt and freshly ground black pepper
- 3 tablespoons Mayonnaise
- 3 tablespoons plain yogurt
- Lettuce leaves
- 1 16-ounce can sliced beets
- ½ cup Vinaigrette
- 2 tablespoons capers

Sprinkle the cucumber slices with salt and place in a strainer or colander in the sink for 30 minutes to wilt. Flatten the chicken breasts slightly. Warm a skillet and add the butter. Add the chicken and cook 1 minute on each side. Add the vermouth and season with the salt and pepper. Cover and cook over medium heat for 10 minutes. Remove the chicken and let it cool. Off the heat, add the mayonnaise and yogurt to the pan juices and mix until smooth. If the sauce becomes too thick, add a little chicken stock or white wine. Let cool.

Line a platter with the lettuce. Cut the chicken into strips and place on the lettuce. Toss the beets with the vinaigrette. Pour the sauce over the chicken and surround it with the wilted cucumbers and beets vinaigrette. Sprinkle with the capers.

Chicken Cacciatore

(4–6 servings)

- 1 large or 2 small chickens, cut into serving pieces
- ¼ cup olive oil
- 1 onion, chopped
- ½ pound mushrooms, sliced
- 1 10-ounce can tomatoes
- ½ cup chicken stock
- ½ cup white wine
- 1 bouquet garni: parsley, bay leaf, and thyme tied in cheesecloth
- Salt and freshly ground black pepper
- 1 clove garlic, crushed

In a large skillet brown the chicken pieces in the oil; reserve. Add the onion to the pan and cook until it is golden. Add the mushrooms and cook for 5 minutes. Add the remaining ingredients, bring to a boil, and return the chicken to the pan (uncovered). Cook for 45 minutes or until the chicken is tender. Serve with rice or spaghetti.

Exotic Chicken Salad

(6 servings)

- ½ cup white wine
- 1 1-inch piece fresh ginger, coarsely chopped
- 1 shallot
- 1 bay leaf
- 3 chicken breasts, split, boned, and skinned
- 2 firm apples, diced
- 1 medium cucumber, peeled, seeded, and diced
- 1 tablespoon capers
- ½ cup Mayonnaise *or* yogurt, *or* ¼ cup of each

In a skillet large enough to hold the chicken in one layer, place the wine, ginger, shallot, and bay leaf. Cook for 1 minute, then add the chicken. Bring to a boil and cover. Simmer until just done, about 10 minutes depending on the thickness of the chicken breasts. Cool the chicken and dice.

Combine the remaining ingredients with the chicken and serve in scallop shells or scooped-out pineapple halves as a luncheon dish.

Chicken or Turkey Tetrazzini

(8 servings)

- ¾ pound mushrooms, sliced
- 4 tablespoons butter
- 3 tablespoons flour
- 2 cups chicken stock
- ½ cup white wine
- Salt and freshly ground white pepper
- ½ cup cream
- ½ pound thin spaghetti, cooked *al dente*
- 3 cups diced cooked chicken *or* turkey
- Grated Parmesan cheese

Preheat the oven to 350°.

In a saucepan cook the mushrooms slowly over low heat in 2 tablespoons of the butter. Add the remaining butter, stir in the flour, and cook for 1 minute. Slowly add the stock, stirring until thickened. Add the wine, cream, and salt and pepper to taste. Add half the sauce to the spaghetti and arrange it in a flat ovenproof dish, leaving a depression in the center for the chicken. Mix the chicken with the remaining sauce and place in the center of the casserole. Sprinkle with the Parmesan and bake until golden (about 30 minutes).

Note: If preparing ahead, do not combine the ingredients until ready to bake; otherwise the spaghetti will absorb the sauce.

Turkey Breast Tonnato

(8–10 servings)

- 1 5-pound turkey breast, boned and rolled
- 2 onions, sliced
- 2 carrots
- 1 celery stalk
- 1 bouquet garni: thyme, bay leaf, and parsley stems tied in cheesecloth
- Salt
- 8 black peppercorns
- Capers (garnish)
- Lemon slices (garnish)

Tuna Sauce:
- 2 7-ounce cans solid white tuna, cold
- 8 anchovy fillets
- 1 cup olive oil
- 3 tablespoons capers
- 3 tablespoons lemon juice
- Salt and freshly ground white pepper

Place the turkey in a large pot, cover with water, and add all the other ingredients (except the garnishes). Bring to a boil and simmer for 1 hour. Let the turkey cool in the liquid, then remove. Cut into thin slices.

To make the sauce: Mash the tuna and anchovies with some of the oil until a smooth paste is formed. (This is easily done in a blender or food processor.) Add the rest of the oil, bit by bit. Then add the capers, lemon juice, and salt and pepper to taste. The sauce should be the consistency of heavy cream. If necessary, thin it with a little cooking liquid from the turkey.

Arrange the turkey slices on a platter, pour the sauce over them, cover platter with plastic wrap, and refrigerate for 24 hours so the meat will absorb the flavor of the sauce. Serve at room temperature, garnished with capers and lemon slices.

Maurice Moore-Betty's Turkey Scallopine with Marsala

(6 servings)

12	slices raw turkey breast (1½–2 pounds), cut ¼ inch thick across the grain
1	cup flour mixed with 5 or 6 twists of pepper from a pepper mill and 2 teaspoons salt
2	tablespoons butter
2	tablespoons oil
¼	pound mushrooms, stems removed, thinly sliced
1	cup chicken stock
¼–½	cup dry Marsala
2	teaspoons cornstarch mixed with about 1 tablespoon water
2	tablespoons finely chopped parsley (garnish)

Lay the turkey slices between two sheets of waxed paper and pound them gently until they are quite thin. Dredge in the seasoned flour; shake off any excess. In a heavy skillet heat the butter and the oil. Sauté the turkey quickly on each side, about 3 or 4 minutes in all for each batch. Keep warm until all have been browned. Sauté the mushrooms in the same fat for 2 to 3 minutes. Remove from the pan with a slotted spoon and add to the turkey; keep warm.

Add the chicken stock to the pan. Raise the heat and cook for 3 to 4 minutes, scraping the bottom of the pan to loosen the browned bits. Add the Marsala and boil for a moment, then add the cornstarch mixture, stirring until the sauce simmers and is smooth and thick. Correct the seasoning, if necessary, with salt and pepper. Pour (or strain) the sauce over the turkey and mushrooms. Garnish with the chopped parsley.

Note: The finished dish freezes successfully.

Game Hens with Cherries

(4 servings)

4	ounces wild rice *or* a mixture of white and wild rice
1½	teaspoons chopped chives *or* chopped onion (or more to taste)
1½	teaspoons chopped parsley
	Salt and freshly ground black pepper
4	Rock Cornish game hens
3	tablespoons butter, softened
½	teaspoon sage
½	teaspoon rosemary
½	teaspoon thyme
1	8-ounce can pitted black cherries

Preheat the oven to 450°.

Cook the rice; mix it with the chives, parsley, and salt and pepper to taste. Stuff the hens with the rice mixture and tie them closed. Rub the hens with the butter, sage, rosemary, thyme, salt, and pepper. Place them side by side in a roasting pan and brown for 15 minutes. Reduce the heat to 350° and bake for 20 minutes. Pour the cherries with their juice over the hens and cook for 20 additional minutes or until tender, basting frequently.

Chicken Livers with Onions & Artichoke Hearts

(4 servings)

    1 pound chicken livers
    1 tablespoon flour
    2 tablespoons butter
    1 16-ounce can whole white onions
    1 16-ounce can artichoke hearts
    ½ cup sherry
    ¼ cup water
    Salt and freshly ground black pepper

Pat the chicken livers dry and sprinkle with the flour. Melt the butter in a large skillet and sauté the livers quickly, turning once. Drain the onions and artichoke hearts, pat dry, and add to the livers. Brown the vegetables for about 2 minutes. Add the sherry, water, and salt and pepper. Cover the skillet and cook over low heat for 10 minutes. Serve with rice or noodles.

Beef, Lamb, Pork & Veal

Chili con Carne
Lazy Beef Stew
The Russian Tea Room's Beef
   Stroganoff
Hungarian Goulash
Jean Anderson's Mushroom & Shallot
   Stuffed Hamburgers
Lynn's Lasagna
Joan Itoh's Sukiyaki Donburi
Réchauffé of Lamb
Stuffed Lamb Portuguese
Roast Lamb with Mustard & Ginger
Grilled Butterflied Lamb
Mixed Grill
Ragout of Lamb
Souvlakia
Moussaka
Venetian Calves' Liver
Jean Anderson's Anatolian Roast Loin
   of Pork with Cinnamon

Roast Loin of Pork with Prunes
Choucroute Garnie
Chinese Spareribs
Pork Chops with Mustard
Pork Chops Charcutière
Sausage, Zucchini & Eggplant
   Casserole
Casserole-roasted Veal
Blanquette de Veau
Ragout of Veal & Eggplant
Elizabeth Esterling's Veal Scallops
   with Artichoke Hearts
Veal Scallops with Orange
Veal Rolls with Tomato Sauce
Jean Anderson's Wheaten Veal Chops
   with Lemon & Capers
Richard Lavin's Peasant Loaf

Chili con Carne

(8 servings)

½ pound dried kidney beans
1 32-ounce can tomato juice (or more if necessary)
2 tablespoons butter
2 medium onions, chopped
3 pounds ground beef
Salt and freshly ground black pepper
1 small (5-ounce) can tomato paste
3 teaspoons sugar
5 tablespoons chili powder
Tabasco sauce

Soak the beans overnight in 1 quart of tomato juice. In a large skillet melt the butter and cook the onion until it is soft. Add the beef and cook until it begins to brown. Add the salt, pepper, tomato paste, sugar, and chili powder. Cook over low heat for 2 hours or until the beans are soft. Add tomato juice if more liquid is needed. Refrigerate overnight. Reheat before serving, adding more tomato juice and the Tabasco as desired.

Lazy Beef Stew

(4 servings)

2 pounds stewing beef, cut in 1-inch cubes
4 carrots, cut in 2-inch lengths
8 small white onions
2 stalks celery, sliced
½ pound mushrooms, sliced
1 envelope onion soup mix
1 10½-ounce can beef broth *or* stock
1 10¾-ounce can tomato soup
4 small potatoes, cut in half (optional)

Combine all the ingredients except the potatoes in an ovenproof casserole. Bake at 300° for 3 hours. If desired, add the potatoes for the last hour of cooking. Add more stock, if needed, during the cooking.

The Russian Tea Room's Beef Stroganoff

(4–6 servings)

- 2 pounds lean boneless sirloin *or* bottom round, in one piece, trimmed of fat and gristle
- 2 teaspoons salt
- ½ teaspoon freshly ground black pepper
- 4 tablespoons butter
- 1 medium onion, thinly sliced
- 1 tablespoon flour
- 1 teaspoon powdered yellow mustard *or* 1 tablespoon prepared Dijon mustard
- ½ cup dry white wine
- 2 teaspoons tomato paste (optional)
- 1 tablespoon minced onion
- ½ pound mushrooms, thinly sliced
- 2 tablespoons dry white wine
- 1 cup sour cream, preferably warmed

Cut the meat into ½-inch-thick slices. Place between two sheets of waxed paper and pound with a mallet or a heavy plate until the meat is ¼ inch thick. Be careful not to tear the meat. Cut the meat into ½- by 2-inch slices. Place the slices in one layer on a large platter. Sprinkle with the salt and pepper and let stand at room temperature for 15 minutes. Heat 2 tablespoons of the butter in a deep, heavy frying pan or shallow saucepan large enough to hold all the ingredients. Add the sliced onion and cook over medium heat, stirring constantly, for about 5 minutes, until the onion begins to soften. Add the meat to the pan. Cook for 3 minutes, turning the slices constantly to brown them evenly. Stir in the flour and mustard and cook, stirring constantly, for 1 more minute. Add the ½ cup of wine and the tomato paste (if desired). Reduce the heat to low, cover the pan, and simmer for 5 to 10 minutes, stirring frequently.

In another frying pan, heat the remaining 2 tablespoons of butter. Add the minced onion and the mushrooms. Cook over medium heat for 2 minutes, add the 2 tablespoons of wine and cook for 2 more minutes; the mushrooms should be firm. Add the mushrooms and their liquid to the meat. Check the seasoning and stir in the sour cream. Simmer over the lowest possible heat for about 5 minutes, just to heat the dish through. Do not boil. Serve over a bed of hot cooked rice or kasha, with a green vegetable on the side.

Hungarian Goulash

(6 servings)

2 pounds beef, cut in 1-inch cubes
3 tablespoons oil
3 large onions, sliced
1½ tablespoons paprika
1½ tablespoons flour
1½ tablespoons tomato paste
2½ cups beef stock or broth
Bouquet garni: bay leaf, thyme, and parsley stems tied in cheesecloth
1 clove garlic, minced (optional)
Salt and freshly ground black pepper
3 large tomatoes, peeled, seeded, and chopped
1 2-ounce jar pimiento, cut into strips
4 tablespoons sour cream, warmed

Preheat the oven to 325°.

In a heavy heatproof casserole with a lid brown the meat in the oil. Remove from the pan and reserve. Add the onion to the pan and brown; add the paprika and flour and cook for 1 minute. Add the tomato paste and return the meat to the pan. Add the stock to cover; add the bouquet garni, garlic, and the salt and pepper. Place aluminum foil over the meat and cover with the lid. Bake for 1½ hours, until tender.

To serve, cover with the chopped tomatoes and pimiento strips and dot with the sour cream.

Jean Anderson's Mushroom & Shallot Stuffed Hamburgers

(4 servings)

1½ pounds lean ground beef chuck
2 tablespoons dry red wine
1 teaspoon Worcestershire sauce
1 teaspoon salt
¼ teaspoon freshly ground black pepper
3 tablespoons unsalted butter
½ cup finely minced fresh mushrooms
2 large shallots, peeled and minced

Combine the meat with the wine, Worcestershire, salt and pepper and shape into 8 thin patties of uniform size. Set aside. Melt 2 tablespoons of the butter in a small, heavy skillet over moderate heat, add the mushrooms and shallots, and stir-fry for about 5 minutes or until most of the juices have cooked away. Spread this mixture on half the patties, dividing the total amount evenly. Top with the remaining patties, then pinch the edges together to enclose the mushrooms and shallots. Heat the remaining 1 tablespoon butter in a large heavy skillet over moderately high heat. Brown the hamburgers for 5 minutes on a side for rare, 6 for medium, and 7 for well done. Or, if you prefer, broil the hamburgers 3 inches from the heat, allowing approximately the same cooking times per side.

Lynn's Lasagna

(6–8 servings)

- ¾ cup chopped onion
- 2 tablespoons olive oil
- 1 pound ground beef
- ½ pound Italian sausage, removed from its casing
- 1 1-pound can tomatoes
- 1 15-ounce can tomato sauce
- 1 clove garlic, minced
- 3 tablespoons parsley flakes
- 2 tablespoons sugar
- 2 teaspoons salt
- 1 teaspoon dried basil
- 2 teaspoons dried oregano
- 1 8-ounce package lasagna noodles
- 3 cups ricotta cheese
- 1 cup grated Parmesan cheese
- ¾ pound mozzarella cheese
- 2 eggs, beaten

In a large skillet cook the onion in the oil until it starts to wilt. Add the beef and sausage and cook until they lose their red color. Drain off the fat. Add the tomatoes, tomato sauce, garlic, 2 tablespoons of the parsley, the sugar, 1 teaspoon of the salt, the basil, and 1 teaspoon of the oregano. Simmer, uncovered, for 1 hour.

Cook noodles according to package directions. In a large bowl combine the ricotta, ½ cup of the Parmesan, and the remaining 1 teaspoon oregano, 1 tablespoon parsley, 1 teaspoon salt, and the eggs.

Preheat the oven to 350°.

Make 3 complete layers of the ingredients in a rectangular baking dish in the following order: Start with the sauce, then the noodles, then the cheese mixture and slices of mozzarella. Finish with the sauce and the remaining Parmesan. Bake for 45 minutes. Let stand 15 minutes before cutting into squares to serve.

Mushroom Lasagna: Follow this recipe but do not use beef or sausage. Instead, increase the amount of onion to 1 cup. When the sauce has cooked for ½ hour, add 1 pound mushrooms that have been thinly sliced and lightly sautéed. Proceed with the rest of the recipe.

Joan Itoh's Sukiyaki Donburi

(4 servings)

    1 block of tofu, about 10 ounces
    2 tablespoons oil
    4 onions, chopped
    2 ounces carrots, minced
    2 ounces *shiitake* mushrooms, cut into
       strips
    4 ounces boneless flank or round steak,
       cut into strips
    2 tablespoons *shoyu*
    Pinch of salt
    1 tablespoon sugar
    2 eggs, beaten
    2 cups freshly cooked rice

Squeeze out any excess liquid from the tofu. Heat the oil in a skillet and add the onions, carrot, and mushrooms. Fry, adding the beef when the onions begin to look golden. Cook for about 2 minutes, then add the tofu. Stir gently to blend. Season with the *shoyu*, salt, and sugar, mix, and remove from the heat. Fan and stir to cool for a few minutes. Stir in the eggs and return the pan to the heat. Cook until the eggs begin to set. Fill four individual bowls with steaming rice. Divide the large omelette, putting one part gently over each bowl of rice. Cover the bowls.

Notes: The raw beef will be easier to slice if you freeze it slightly first.

A *donburi* bowl is larger than a rice bowl and has a cover. This is a very popular meal in Japan and a great many combinations of food can go over the rice. *Donburi* is almost always served with a side dish of various Japanese pickles.

Réchauffé of Lamb

(2–3 servings)

    2 tablespoons olive oil
    ½ cup chopped onions
    2 cups leftover cooked lamb, cut into
       small cubes
    ½ cup red wine
    Leftover gravy

In a skillet heat the olive oil and sauté the onion until golden. Add the meat and brown quickly on all sides. Add the wine, bring to a boil, stirring, and add the gravy. Taste for seasonings. Serve over rice.

Note: I've been doing this with leftover lamb since I was a teenager; I raved over this dish in a small New York French restaurant and was given the recipe.

Stuffed Lamb Portuguese

(6–8 servings)

Stuffing:

 1 tablespoon butter
 1 medium onion, finely chopped
 4 ounces ground walnuts
 Crumbs made from 2 slices fresh white bread
 1 tablespoon chopped parsley
 Zest of ½ lemon
 Juice of ½ lemon
 1 egg, beaten
 Salt and freshly ground black pepper

 1 leg of lamb (6–7 pounds), boned
 1 cup white wine
 1 tablespoon arrowroot mixed with ½ cup water

In a skillet melt the butter and sauté the onion until it is transparent. In a bowl combine the onion with the remaining stuffing ingredients.

Preheat the oven to 450°.

Place the stuffing mixture on the boned lamb, roll, and tie securely. Place the roll in a small roasting pan. Pour the wine around it to a depth of ½ inch. Roast for 15 minutes. Reduce the heat to 350° and cook for 25 minutes per pound of meat, basting often with the pan juices. Remove the lamb to a platter and let cool slightly. Degrease the pan juices and thicken slightly with the arrowroot paste. Slice the lamb and serve. Pass the gravy in a warm sauceboat.

Roast Lamb with Mustard & Ginger

(8–10 servings)

 ½ cup Dijon mustard
 2 tablespoons soy sauce
 2 cloves garlic, crushed
 1 tablespoon fresh ginger, minced, or ½ teaspoon ground
 2 tablespoons olive oil
 1 leg of lamb (6–7 pounds)

Beat the mustard, soy sauce, garlic, and ginger with a whisk, then add the oil drop by drop. Paint the lamb with this mixture and let it stand at room temperature for several hours. Bake at 350° for 1½ hours for medium-rare meat.

Grilled Butterflied Lamb

(6–8 servings)

Mint Sauce:

- ¼ cup sugar
- ⅓ cup water
- ½ cup white vinegar
- ¾ cup fresh mint leaves, chopped

- 1 leg of lamb (7–8 pounds), boned and butterflied

Combine the sugar, water, and vinegar in a small saucepan. Bring to a boil and simmer for 3 minutes. Pour the liquid over the mint and let cool.

Put the lamb in a flat pan and pour the mint sauce over it. Marinate for a few hours at room temperature (or overnight in the refrigerator). Grill over charcoal or broil for about 10–12 minutes on each side, depending on the thickness.

Note: The meat will not be of uniform thickness, so you can serve all tastes, from medium rare to well done. Don't overcook it. You can use a bottle of commercial mint sauce if you wish.

Mixed Grill

For each person:

- 1 rib lamb chop
- 1 sausage
- 1 lamb kidney
- ½ tomato
- 2 mushroom caps
- Salt and freshly ground black pepper
- Butter
- Watercress (garnish)

Preheat the oven to 400°.

Rub the chops and kidneys with salt and pepper. Broil, barbecue, or sauté until done, turning once. At the same time place the tomatoes and mushrooms in a baking pan, dot with butter, and season with salt and pepper. Bake for 6 to 8 minutes. Arrange the meats and vegetables on a platter and garnish with the watercress. A baked potato is a welcome addition.

Ragout of Lamb

(6 servings)

- 4 tablespoons butter (or more if needed)
- 3 pounds lamb shoulder, cut into 1-inch cubes
- 6 carrots, peeled and cut into 1-inch pieces
- 4 white turnips, peeled and cut into 1-inch pieces
- 1 pound small white onions
- ½ pound mushrooms, cut in half
- 3 tablespoons flour
- ½ cup red wine
- 1 cup stock
- Salt and freshly ground black pepper
- 1 1-pound can peeled tomatoes
- 1 package frozen string beans
- 1 package frozen peas
- Chopped parsley (garnish)

In a large skillet melt 2 tablespoons of the butter and brown the meat quickly; remove and set aside. Adding more butter if necessary, quickly brown the carrots, turnips, onions, and mushrooms. Melt the remaining 2 tablespoons butter, remove the pan from the heat and stir in the flour. Return to the heat for a minute and add the wine and stock, stirring until thickened. Return the meat to the pan and add salt and pepper to taste. Bring to a boil and simmer for 45 minutes. Add the tomatoes with some of their juice and the string beans. Cook for 10 more minutes. Add the peas and cook for another 5 minutes. Taste for seasonings and adjust if necessary. Sprinkle with the chopped parsley before serving.

Variation: You may add pieces of potato before the last 30 minutes of cooking time.

Souvlakia

(6 servings)

- ¼ cup olive oil
- Zest of 1 lemon, grated
- Juice of ½ lemon
- 2 garlic cloves, crushed
- 1 teaspoon oregano
- 1 tablespoon Dijon mustard
- 2 pounds lean lamb, cut into 2-inch cubes
- Bay leaves

Combine the first 6 ingredients and marinate the lamb in the mixture for at least 1 hour. Pat the meat dry and thread it onto skewers, adding pieces of bay leaf between the meat. Cook quickly over hot charcoal, turning often. The meat should be brown on the outside, juicy and pink inside. Serve with a Greek salad of cucumbers, tomatoes, black olives, and feta cheese.

Moussaka

(8 servings)

3 pounds unpeeled eggplant, cut lengthwise into ½-inch slices
Salt
Olive oil
1 medium onion, minced
2 pounds ground lamb or beef or turkey
1 1-pound can tomatoes, drained and chopped, juice reserved
2 tablespoons chopped parsley
¼ teaspoon cinnamon
¼ teaspoon nutmeg
4 ounces dry red wine
4 ounces or more kefalotyri or Parmesan cheese, freshly grated

Béchamel Sauce:

4 ounces butter
4 tablespoons flour
3 cups milk
Salt and freshly ground black pepper
Nutmeg
3 eggs, beaten well

Sprinkle the eggplant slices with salt and drain on paper towels for at least 30 minutes. Rinse well and pat dry with more paper towels. Sauté the eggplant in the olive oil until brown on both sides. Reserve. (You may prefer to brush the slices with olive oil and brown under the broiler, which is faster.) In a large skillet, sauté the onion in 2 tablespoons of the olive oil until soft. Add the meat and tomatoes. When the meat begins to brown, add the parsley, cinnamon, nutmeg, red wine, and a little juice from the tomatoes. Simmer for 20 minutes over medium heat.

Preheat the oven to 350°.

Make the Béchamel sauce while the meat is simmering. Melt the butter, remove from the heat, stir in the flour, return to the heat, and cook for 1 minute. Gradually add the milk, stirring continuously until the sauce thickens. Add the salt, pepper, and nutmeg to taste. Mix ½ cup of the sauce with the meat. In a well-greased 9- by 13-inch ovenproof dish layer the eggplant slices, meat sauce, and sprinklings of cheese, finishing with a layer of eggplant. Add the eggs to the remaining sauce and pour it over the eggplant. Sprinkle with additional cheese and bake for 1 hour. Allow to stand for 20 minutes before serving; it will then cut easily into squares.

Note: This dish reheats well.

Venetian Calves' Liver

(3–4 servings)

- 4 tablespoons olive oil
- 3 medium onions, sliced thinly
- ¼ teaspoon dried sage
- 1 pound calves' liver, cut across in ¼-inch strips
  Salt and freshly ground black pepper
- ¼ cup white wine
  Chopped parsley (garnish)

Heat 2 tablespoons of the olive oil in a skillet. Add the onions and cook until golden. Add the sage and cook for 2 more minutes, until soft. In another skillet, heat the remaining 2 tablespoons of olive oil. Dry the liver strips on paper towels, sprinkle with the salt and pepper, and sauté in the oil for 2 or 3 minutes, turning often. When the liver is lightly browned, add the onions and cook for 1 to 2 more minutes. Remove the liver to a heated platter and deglaze the pan with the white wine. Pour this sauce over the liver and sprinkle with the parsley.

Jean Anderson's Anatolian Roast Loin of Pork with Cinnamon

(8–10 servings)

- 1 boned and rolled loin of pork (4–5 pounds)
- 2 tablespoons unsalted butter, at room temperature
- 2 large garlic cloves, peeled and crushed
- ½ teaspoon ground cinnamon
- ½ teaspoon crumbled leaf rosemary
- ¼ teaspoon crumbled leaf thyme
- ½ teaspoon salt
- ¼ teaspoon freshly ground black pepper

Rub the pork well all over with a mixture of the remaining ingredients. Place on a rack in a shallow roasting pan and let stand 1 hour at room temperature. Roast in a 350° oven, allowing 35 to 40 minutes per pound or until a meat thermometer registers 170°. Do not cover the roast at any time and do not add liquid to the pan. When the meat is done, remove the roast from the oven and let stand 30 minutes. Remove the strings, place on a heated platter, and serve.

Note: Boneless roasts, of course, are a cinch to carve. But if you have chosen a bone-in roast, ask the butcher to crack the backbone at the base of each rib so that the carver need only slice between the ribs, allotting 1 to 2 chops per person. For a bone-in roast, allow 30 to 35 minutes per pound.

Roast Loin of Pork with Prunes

(6–8 servings)

1 boneless loin of pork (3½ pounds), with the bones reserved
16 pitted prunes (if not moist, soak for 1 hour in hot tea)
Salt and freshly ground black pepper
½ cup Madeira
½ cup water
1 tablespoon arrowroot mixed with ¼ cup water

Preheat the oven to 375°.

Using a knife with a long thin blade, run it through the middle of the pork loin (lengthwise) to make a pocket for the prunes. (You may have to do this from each end rather than in one stroke.) Drain the prunes and insert them into the pocket with your fingers. Tie the pork with string to retain its shape and keep the pocket closed. Season with the salt and pepper.

Put the pork in a shallow roasting pan, fat side up, and surround it with the reserved bones. Roast for 2 hours, turning every 15 minutes. Remove the meat to a platter and keep warm. Discard the bones, pour off the fat, and add the wine and water to the brown bits that have collected in the pan. Bring it to a boil and add salt and pepper to taste if needed. Strain the gravy and thicken with the arrowroot mixture. Slice the pork and serve with the gravy.

Choucroute Garnie

(4–6 servings)

- 4 lean pork chops, ½ inch thick, trimmed of fat
- 2 tablespoons corn oil
- 2 pounds sauerkraut, rinsed with cold water and drained
- 12 juniper berries
- 12 white peppercorns
- 4 frankfurters
- ½ pound ham steak, cut into 4 pieces
- White wine
- 6 new potatoes, boiled and kept warm

In an ovenproof enamel casserole lightly brown the chops in the oil. Remove the chops and set aside. Place the sauerkraut in the pan and add the juniper and pepper. Bury all the meats in the sauerkraut and cover with the wine. Cover the casserole with aluminum foil and then with the lid. Cook in a 325° oven for 2½ hours.

Mound the sauerkraut on a hot platter and put the meats and boiled potatoes around it. Serve with Dijon mustard.

Chinese Spareribs

(3–4 servings)

- 3 pounds spareribs, cut into ribs
- 1 lemon, sliced thin

Sauce:
- ½ cup dry cocktail sherry
- 1 tablespoon brown sugar
- 2 tablespoons soy sauce
- 1 tablespoon sesame oil

Preheat the oven to 350°.

Cut the spareribs into serving pieces if the ribs are large and place on a rack in a roasting pan. Place the lemon slices over the meat and bake for 1 hour, turning the ribs once. While the ribs are baking, combine the sauce ingredients. Pour out all the fat from the pan. Remove the rack and return the ribs to the pan. Brush the ribs with the sauce and return the pan to the oven for 10 minutes. Turn the ribs and brush with the remaining sauce. Return to oven for 10 more minutes or until brown.

Pork Chops with Mustard

(3–4 servings)

4   tablespoons flour
Salt and freshly ground black pepper
6   center-cut pork chops 1 inch thick
2   tablespoons butter
3   tablespoons oil
1½   cups sliced onions
¼   cup tarragon vinegar *or* wine vinegar
Chicken stock *or* water
Bouquet garni: parsley, thyme, and a
      bay leaf tied in cheesecloth
½   cup heavy cream *or* crème fraîche
2   teaspoons Dijon mustard
Few drops lemon juice
Parsley (garnish)

Preheat the oven to 325°.

Season the flour with the salt and pepper and lightly flour the chops. Melt the butter and oil in a large skillet and quickly brown the chops, removing them to a flat casserole large enough to hold them in one layer. Add the onions to the pan and cook until soft and golden. Deglaze the pan with the vinegar, stirring to pick up the brown bits on the bottom. If the mixture is too dry, add a little chicken stock or water. Spoon the onions and pan juices over the chops and add the bouquet garni. Bring the casserole to a boil on top of the stove, then bake for 15 minutes.

Baste with the pan juices, adding more chicken stock or water if there is not enough liquid. Bake for another 15 minutes, turn the chops, and bake for 5 minutes more. Test for doneness near the bone.

When the chops are done, place them on a heated platter. Remove as much fat as possible from the pan juices and return the casserole to the heat. Add the cream and bring to a boil, stirring constantly until the sauce coats the back of a spoon. Remove from the heat, add the mustard and lemon juice, and stir to combine. Strain the sauce through a fine sieve. Pour over the chops, garnish with parsley, and serve.

Pork Chops Charcutière

(6 servings)

- 6 center-cut pork chops, 1 inch thick
- 3 tablespoons oil
- 1 tablespoon butter
- 2 medium onions, chopped
- 1 tablespoon flour
- ¼ teaspoon dried thyme
- 1 bay leaf
- 1 1-pound can tomatoes, drained and chopped
- Salt and freshly ground black pepper
- ½ cup vermouth
- ½ cup beef stock *or* bouillon
- 2 tablespoons chopped sour pickles
- 1 tablespoon capers

Preheat the oven to 325°.

Trim the fat from the chops and brown them quickly in the oil, using a heavy heatproof casserole. Remove the chops and pour off the fat. Lower the heat, add the butter to the pan, and cook the onion until it is soft but not brown. Sprinkle on the flour and stir for 1 minute. Add the herbs, tomatoes, and salt and pepper and cook for 5 minutes, stirring often. Add the vermouth and stock and simmer for 10 minutes. Place the chops, overlapping, in a casserole, and spoon the sauce over them. Bake, covered, for 30 minutes. Add the pickles and capers just before serving.

Sausage, Zucchini & Eggplant Casserole

(6 servings)

- 1 large or 2 small eggplants, cut into ½-inch slices
- Salt
- 1 dozen sweet Italian sausages, cut into 1-inch pieces
- 5 small white onions, peeled and sliced
- ½ pound fresh mushrooms, sliced
- 1 8-ounce can tomato purée
- 1 4-ounce can tomato sauce
- ¼ teaspoon oregano
- 1 clove garlic, minced
- 1 bay leaf
- Freshly ground black pepper
- Vegetable oil
- 5 small zucchini, cut into ½-inch slices
- ½ pint cottage cheese
- ¼ cup grated Parmesan cheese

Preheat the oven to 350°.

Sprinkle the eggplant slices with salt and drain on paper towels for 20 minutes. In an ovenproof casserole over low heat cook the sausage with ½ cup of water for 10 minutes, covered. Pour off all the fat and water, add the onions, and cook until they are soft. Add the mushrooms and cook for 5 minutes more. Add the tomato purée, tomato sauce, and spices. Simmer for 5 minutes. Rinse the eggplant slices and pat dry. Brush them with oil and broil on both sides until brown. Remove half of the sauce from the casserole. Put the eggplant on top of the remaining sauce. Spread the cottage cheese on the eggplant and sprinkle with half of the Parmesan. Finish with a layer of the zucchini, the remaining sauce, and then the rest of the Parmesan. Bake for 30 minutes. Let cool slightly before serving.

Vegetarian Variation: Simply omit the sausage from the recipe, cooking the onions and mushrooms in the casserole in 1 or 2 tablespoons of butter.

Melt the butter in a heavy casserole that has a lid, add the veal, and surround it with the onion. Bake for 10 minutes. Reduce the heat to 325 °. Scatter the potatoes around the meat and tuck the garlic under the meat if desired. Season with salt and pepper to taste. Add the stock, cover with aluminum foil and then with the lid. Cook for 2 hours, removing the lid and foil for the last 15 minutes to allow the top to brown. Let the meat sit for 10 minutes before carving. Discard the garlic. Slice the veal on a platter, and surround with the potatoes and onions. Spoon over some of the juices and pass the rest in a sauceboat.

Casserole-roasted Veal

(8 servings)

    4 pounds veal shoulder, boned and
       rolled
Salt and freshly ground pepper
    1 teaspoon dried rosemary
    2 tablespoons butter
    2 onions, cut into ⅛-inch slices
    6 potatoes, peeled and cut into
       ⅛-inch slices
    2 cloves garlic (optional)
    ½ cup chicken, veal, *or* beef stock

Preheat the oven to 450 °.
    Rub the veal with the salt, pepper, and rosemary (or a mixture of herbs if desired).

Blanquette de Veau

(6 servings)

2½   pounds veal shoulder, cut into
      1-by-2-inch pieces
1   carrot, sliced
1   onion, stuck with 4 cloves
1   stalk celery, sliced
6   peppercorns
Bouquet garni: thyme, bay leaf, and
      parsley stems tied in cheesecloth
Salt
5   tablespoons butter
3   tablespoons flour
12–14 small white onions
½   pound mushrooms
2   egg yolks
½   cup cream
1   teaspoon lemon juice
Salt and freshly ground white pepper
Chopped parsley (garnish)

Place the veal in a heavy enamel pan and cover with cold water. Bring slowly to a boil and skim the foam from the surface. Add the carrot, onion, celery, peppercorns, bouquet garni, and salt. Cover and simmer for 1 hour, until the meat is tender. Allow the meat to stand in the stock.

In a saucepan, prepare a white sauce with 3 tablespoons of the butter, the flour, and 2 cups of the strained veal stock. Allow the sauce to simmer for 10 to 15 minutes. Cut the ends from the onions and cut an *x* on each root end to keep them from falling apart. Place the onions in a saucepan, cover with water, and bring to a boil. Boil the onions for 1 minute and refresh under cold water. Remove onions and peel; the peels will slide off easily. Sauté the onions in 1 tablespoon of the remaining butter until golden. Remove the onions and reserve. Add the remaining 2 tablespoons butter to the pan and sauté the mushrooms.

Remove the meat from the stock with a slotted spoon and add to the white sauce along with the onions and mushrooms. Allow the *blanquette* to simmer for a few minutes. In a separate bowl, beat the egg yolks, cream, and lemon juice together. Slowly add some of the hot *blanquette* sauce to the egg mixture; then add the entire egg mixture to the *blanquette*. Do not allow the sauce to boil after the egg mixture has been added. Serve sprinkled with chopped parsley.

Note: This is an excellent party dish served over rice or noodles.

Ragout of Veal & Eggplant

(6 servings)

- 4 tablespoons olive oil
- 3 pounds lean stewing veal, cut into 2-inch cubes
- 2 large onions, peeled and cut into 1-inch cubes
- 4 tablespoons flour
- 1 large eggplant, unpeeled, cut into 2-inch cubes
- 1 pound zucchini (2 large, 3 or 4 medium), cut into 1-inch slices
- 1 28-ounce can tomatoes, drained and chopped, juice reserved
- 2 cups chicken stock
- 1 cup dry white wine
- Bouquet garni: parsley stems, thyme, a bay leaf, and a garlic clove tied in cheesecloth
- Salt and freshly ground black pepper

Preheat the oven to 350°.

In a large heatproof casserole or skillet, heat the oil and brown the meat on all sides. Add the onion, stirring until it is wilted. Sprinkle in the flour and stir to coat the meat. Add the eggplant and zucchini and stir for 1 minute. Add the tomatoes, stock, wine, and the juice from the tomatoes. Bring to a boil and stir until the sauce has thickened. Add the bouquet garni to the casserole and bake for 1¼ hours. Serve with rice and a green salad.

Elizabeth Esterling's Veal Scallops with Artichoke Hearts

(6 servings)

- 12 veal scallops
- Flour
- 2 6½-ounce jars artichoke hearts in oil, drained, oil reserved
- Salt and freshly ground black pepper
- Lemon juice
- Chopped parsley (garnish)

Remove any filaments, fat, or skin left on the scallops, so that the meat will not curl as it cooks. Place each scallop between 2 sheets of waxed paper and pound lightly. Wrap the scallops in waxed paper and refrigerate until you are ready to cook them.

Flour the scallops very lightly, shaking off any excess. (If done in advance, the flour becomes sticky.) Heat 2 tablespoons of the oil from the artichoke hearts in a skillet, and sauté the veal, a few pieces at a time, for about 4 minutes on each side, adding more oil as needed. Season to taste with the salt and pepper and remove the veal to a warm platter. Add the artichoke hearts to the skillet and cook, stirring gently, until warmed through. Arrange the artichoke hearts on the platter with the veal. Sprinkle with the lemon juice and parsley and serve immediately.

Variation: Use scallops of turkey breast instead of the veal.

Veal Scallops with Orange

(4 servings)

- 2 navel oranges
- 2 tablespoons butter
- 2 tablespoons vegetable oil
- 4 veal scallops
- 1 tablespoon flour
- 1 tablespoon sherry, flamed
- 5 ounces chicken stock

Salt and freshly ground black pepper
Parsley sprigs (garnish)

Grate the zest of 1 orange and reserve; then squeeze the juice, strain, and reserve. With a serrated knife, peel the other orange, making sure to cut away all the white membrane. Slice the orange into rounds, wrap in aluminum foil, and warm in a low oven.

In a skillet, melt the butter in the oil and brown the scallops on both sides. Remove the scallops from the pan and stir in the flour, orange zest, strained orange juice, flamed sherry, and the stock. Season to taste with salt and pepper. Bring the sauce to a boil, stirring. Return the veal to the pan and simmer for 10 minutes, covered. Serve garnished with the warmed orange slices and parsley.

Veal Rolls with Tomato Sauce

(4 servings)

- ½ pound Italian sweet sausage, removed from its casing
- ½ clove garlic, crushed
- ½ cup finely chopped onion
- 1 tablespoon chopped parsley
- 1 egg

Salt and freshly ground black pepper
- 4 large veal scallops, pounded as thin as possible
- 2 tablespoons butter

Preheat the oven to 350°.

In a bowl combine the sausage meat with the garlic, onion, parsley, egg, and salt and pepper. Divide the mixture into fourths and place a portion on each veal scallop. Roll each scallop around its stuffing and tie with string. In a low-sided heatproof flat dish (such as a fairly large gratin dish), melt the butter and brown the veal rolls quickly on all sides. Bake for 25 minutes. Remove the strings. Serve with Fresh Tomato Sauce.

Jean Anderson's Wheaten Veal Chops with Lemon & Capers

(4 servings)

- 4 1-inch-thick veal loin or rib chops, each about ⅓–½ pound
- ½ teaspoon salt
- ⅛ teaspoon freshly ground black pepper
- ⅓ cup evaporated milk
- ⅓ cup unsifted whole wheat flour
- 3 tablespoons unsalted butter
- 2 tablespoons peanut or other cooking oil

Juice of ½ large lemon
- 2 tablespoons small capers, well drained

Trim any excess fat from the chops, then season each one well on both sides with the salt and pepper. Dip both sides of the chops into the milk, then dip into the flour until they are well coated. Let the dredged chops stand at room temperature for 10 minutes on a piece of waxed paper; turn carefully and let stand another 10 minutes on a wire rack. This will help the flour to stick.

Heat 1 tablespoon of the butter and all of the oil in a large, heavy skillet over moderately high heat until faint ripples appear in the oil. Add the chops and brown well, about 3 to 4 minutes on the first side. Turn the chops carefully with tongs, reduce the heat to low, and cook very slowly for 15 minutes longer. Remove the chops to a hot platter and keep warm. Pour off all the drippings. To the skillet add the remaining 2 tablespoons butter and raise the heat to moderate. When the butter bubbles and browns (in a minute or two), add the lemon juice and capers and bring just to a boil. Pour over the chops and serve at once.

Richard Lavin's Peasant Loaf

(6 servings)

- 1 large round loaf of Tuscan bread *or* any round crusty bread

Vinaigrette

Basil

Oregano

Thyme

Marjoram

Salt and freshly ground black pepper
- ¼ pound Swiss cheese, very thinly sliced
- ¼ pound provolone, very thinly sliced
- ¼ pound Polish ham, very thinly sliced
- ¼ pound Genoa salami, very thinly sliced
- ¼ pound pepperoni, very thinly sliced
- ¼ pound mortadella, very thinly sliced
- 2 large tomatoes, thinly sliced
- 2 red onions, thinly sliced

Slice off the top of the bread and reserve it to use as a lid. Scoop the soft insides from the bread, leaving only the crust, and save for another use. Brush the vinaigrette over the inside of the crust and sprinkle with the herbs, salt, and pepper to taste. Place the cheeses, meats, tomato slices, and onion slices inside the bread crust in alternating layers — such as Swiss, Genoa salami, provolone, tomato slices, pepperoni, onion slices, mortadella, Polish ham — and repeat until the loaf is full. Replace the top slice on the bread, wrap the loaf tightly in a clean cloth towel, and let sit for 24 hours in the refrigerator. Just before serving, cut the loaf as you would a pie and serve in wedges.

Sauces

Béarnaise Sauce
Quick Aspic
Barbecue Sauce
Elizabeth Esterling's Cucumber Sauce
Elizabeth Esterling's Lemon Sauce
Helen Corbitt's Lemon-Butter Sauce
Mayonnaise
Mornay Sauce
Pesto
Salsa Verde (Green Sauce)
Fresh Tomato Sauce
Vinaigrette

Béarnaise Sauce

(1 cup)

¼ cup tarragon vinegar
¼ cup white wine
2 tablespoons finely chopped shallots
1 teaspoon dried tarragon *or* 1 tablespoon fresh
4 egg yolks
¼ pound butter, softened
Cayenne pepper
Lemon juice
¼ cup boiling water
1 tablespoon finely chopped fresh tarragon *or* parsley

Combine the vinegar, wine, shallots, and tarragon in a small pan (not aluminum). Bring
to a boil and reduce to about 2 tablespoons.
Cool. In the container of a blender or food
processor place the egg yolks, butter, cooled
tarragon mixture, a few grains of cayenne, a
few drops of lemon juice, and the boiling
water. Blend until smooth. Transfer the sauce
to the top of a double boiler; the water in the
bottom of the double boiler must not touch
the upper pot.
   Cook the sauce over medium heat, stirring
with a rubber spatula and scraping the bottom and sides as the sauce begins to thicken.
If the sauce thickens too quickly, remove the
top of the double boiler and continue stirring

off the heat. Add the chopped tarragon or
parsley, taste for seasonings, and place over
warm water until ready to use.

Quick Aspic

(1½ cups)

1 envelope unflavored gelatin
¼ cup water
1 10½-ounce can consommé, with gelatin added
1 tablespoon sherry or Madeira

Sprinkle the gelatin on the water to soften. In
a saucepan heat the consommé and dissolve
the gelatin in it. Add the wine. Chill until
firm.

Note: Use chicken consommé for Deviled
Eggs in Aspic. Beef consommé can be used
for an aspic to mold over individual portions
of cooked meat.

Barbecue Sauce

(2½ cups)

1 cup ketchup *or* chili sauce
1 8-ounce can tomato sauce
1 tablespoon Worcestershire sauce
1 tablespoon A-1 sauce
1 tablespoon mustard
1 tablespoon maple syrup
¼ cup vinegar
Tabasco sauce to taste

Combine all the ingredients in a small sauce-pan and bring to a boil. Simmer for 10 minutes. Coat poultry or meat before barbecuing, roasting, or broiling.

Elizabeth Esterling's Cucumber Sauce

(2 cups)

1 cucumber, peeled, seeded, and grated
1 cup Mayonnaise
1 tablespoon Dijon mustard
1 tablespoon lemon juice
1 tablespoon chopped chives

In a mixing bowl combine all the ingredients, stirring gently. Serve over cold Salmon Loaf or another cold fish dish.

Elizabeth Esterling's Lemon Sauce

(1 cup)

1 tablespoon minced onion
1 tablespoon butter
1 tablespoon flour
¾ cup water with 1 chicken bouillon cube *or* ¾ cup stock
1 tablespoon snipped parsley
½ teaspoon grated lemon peel
1½ tablespoons lemon juice
Freshly ground white pepper

In a skillet cook the onion in the butter until it is soft. Blend in the flour. Stir in the stock. Cook until the sauce is thick, stirring constantly. Add the parsley, lemon peel, lemon juice, and pepper to taste. Serve over hot Salmon Loaf or another fish dish.

Helen Corbitt's Lemon-Butter Sauce

(¼ cup)

    ¼   cup butter
    1   tablespoon chopped parsley
    1   tablespoon lemon juice

Cream the butter and add the parsley and lemon juice. Serve over steak, fish, or vegetables.

Parsley Butter: Add 2 tablespoons chopped parsley to the basic recipe.

Anchovy Butter: Substitute 1½ teaspoons anchovy paste for the parsley.

Mustard Butter: Add 1 teaspoon prepared mustard to the basic recipe. Serve over broiled fish.

Mayonnaise

(1¼ cups)

    1   large egg
    ¾   teaspoon salt
    1   teaspoon Dijon mustard
    1½   teaspoons white wine vinegar
    1   cup salad oil

Using a whisk, blender, or food processor, combine the first 4 ingredients. Add the oil drop by drop at first, then in a steady stream, blending all the while. Do not overprocess.

Variation: For Watercress Mayonnaise, mince finely ¾ cup watercress leaves and combine with the other ingredients before adding the oil.

Mornay Sauce

(1½ cups)

    2 tablespoons butter
    2 tablespoons flour
    1 cup milk
    Salt and freshly ground white pepper
    ½ cup grated Gruyère cheese

In a sauccpan melt the butter over low heat. Stir in the flour and cook for 1 minute. Remove from the heat and stir in the milk. Stir over medium heat until the sauce is thick. Add the salt and pepper to taste. Boil for a few minutes. Remove from the heat and stir in the cheese. Do not reheat the sauce after adding the cheese or it will become stringy.

Pesto

(1 cup)

    1 small clove garlic
    1 cup fresh basil leaves
    ⅓ cup chopped walnuts
    ¼ cup freshly grated Parmesan cheese
    ¼ cup olive oil

Place the first 4 ingredients in a blender or food processor. Blend to combine. With the blender on a low speed, remove the cover and add the oil in a fine stream. Serve with pasta, hot or cold.

Note: This sauce freezes well. When freezing, coat the top with oil to keep it from turning brown.

Salsa Verde
(Green Sauce)

(1 cup)

    1 cup spinach, stems removed
    12 sprigs parsley, stems removed
    12 sprigs watercress, stems removed
    ½ cup olive oil *or* vegetable oil
    Salt and freshly ground black pepper
    1 hard-cooked egg yolk
    1 clove garlic (optional)
    Lemon juice (optional)

Combine all the ingredients in a blender or food processor. Serve with Cold Fish Mousse or any cold boiled meat, fish, or poultry.

Fresh Tomato Sauce

(1½ cups)

- 1 pound fresh tomatoes *or* 1 16-ounce can whole tomatoes
- 1 medium-sized onion, chopped
- ¼ teaspoon dried thyme
- 1 bay leaf
- Salt and freshly ground black pepper
- ¼ cup water (omit if using canned tomatoes)

In a medium-size saucepan combine all the ingredients; cook over medium heat until the tomatoes are soft, 15–20 minutes. Put mixture through a food mill or push through a strainer. Taste for seasonings and adjust if necessary.

Notes: This sauce can be used with Veal Rolls or any other meat or poultry dish for which tomato sauce is an ingredient. It is also a good quick sauce for spaghetti or other pasta.

The recipe can be doubled or otherwise multiplied. Remember to taste for seasoning and make any necessary adjustments.

Vinaigrette

(½–¾ cup)

- 2 teaspoons Dijon mustard
- ¼ teaspoon salt
- Freshly ground black pepper
- 1 tablespoon white wine vinegar *or* lemon juice
- 1 tablespoon warm water
- ¼–½ cup olive oil *or* other vegetable oil *or* a combination

In a mixing bowl combine the first 5 ingredients with a whisk. Add the oil, a little at a time, until it is all incorporated.

Variations: Herbs, garlic, or shallots may be added to taste.

Desserts

Desserts

For many of us, desserts are the stuff of which dreams are made; as children, we looked wistfully to the days when, as adults, we could have all the desserts we craved without first eating a well-balanced meal.

Though today's trend is toward lighter meals and limiting calories, desserts can still be delicious. Many fruit desserts, light soufflés, ices, and sherbets are perfect complements to contemporary cuisine. And we are still fond of the old favorites — the pies and cakes, cookies and ice creams, puddings and sauces, we traditionally serve on special occasions.

In the chapters that follow, you will find selections for the perfect ending to any meal, any season of the year.

Pies are perfect desserts for entertaining since they can always be made ahead of time. In addition to such standards as Pecan Pie, Lemon Pie, and Creamy Coconut Pie, special pies abound. Kentucky Derby Pie, rich with chocolate, pecans, bourbon, and sweetened whipped cream, is easily made in almost no time using a food processor. Easy As Pie makes its own crust. The batter is prepared in the blender, and dessert's in the oven before you know it. The Kiwi Tart is not only trendy, but it can be made with a combination of summer fruits.

A good time to invite children into the kitchen is when you are baking a cake. You can keep them busy handing you ingredients and putting them away (or measuring them, if the children are old enough), and while the cake is in the oven, you can ask your helpers to tidy up the kitchen before it's time to whip up the frosting. Crazy Cupcakes are easy and fun for kids to help with — lots of ingredients to measure, but no complicated preparation.

For grownups, Sallie Y. Williams's Mocha Cake is an elegant dessert, worth the time you'll spend on it. Blueberry-Pineapple Cheesecake is less formal but an equally attractive presentation. Orange Sponge Cake is a perfect dessert for a luncheon, especially topped with Orange Frosting. And Sinfully Rich Cheesecake, with a filling of sour cream, cream cheese, and eggs, is a crowd pleaser for special occasions. Carrot Cake and Poppy Seed Cake are among the more healthful desserts we're enjoying these days.

Cookies, brownies, and meringues are family favorites and fun for company, too. An assortment of cookies is a lovely way to end a meal — lunch or dinner, hearty or light. No-Bake Brownies are especially great in the summer. Meringues can be piped or spooned out in cookie-sized shapes. For a special treat, form them into cups; after baking and cooling, fill them with ice cream and drizzle over a topping or liqueur of your choice. Apricot Bars and Walnut Bars are hearty cookies that make excellent desserts for light meals.

Soufflés and puddings may seem like a challenge if

you haven't tackled many desserts, but many of them are quick and easy. Try "double boiler" soufflés, for instance — they "bake" over boiling water and are virtually foolproof. Though mousses have long been considered elegant desserts, you can make them easily with great success. Chocolate Mousse Chanticleer, a favorite dessert on Nantucket Island, is very easy to make if you have a bit of time. If you don't, try Speedy Chocolate Mousse. For a touch of the unusual, we have included Grand Marnier and Ginger mousses.

Rice Pudding and Bread Pudding, Brown Betty and Trifle, have been American favorites for generations. If they haven't been standard in your family, here they are for you to discover for yourself.

Ice Creams, Sherbets & Ices — wonderful partners for cookies — are desserts that appeal to just about everyone, even the most calorie-conscious. Many of us have given in to the desire to own electric ice cream freezers; the rest of us can make very good ice cream using a metal tray in the freezer compartment of the refrigerator. Though there are recipes here for ice creams of all varieties, including many made with fruit, the only limit is your imagination. Create ices from esoteric fruits for grand finales for luncheons and light suppers. Try kiwi or pomegranate; many greengrocers carry both.

Elizabeth Schneider Colchie's Pineapple Snow is not an ice cream, sherbet, or ice. It's made with pineapple, rum, fine granulated sugar, and cream; when frozen, the mixture is as refreshing as snow.

Fruits of every variety are now available year-round. If the fancy strikes you, Strawberries in Champagne are yours in the dead of winter — for a breakfast or brunch worthy of royalty, or as a dessert to enjoy one berry at a time.

More down to earth, but just as enjoyable, is a dessert of fresh fruit and cheese with wine. Fruit desserts can be elegant, too. Try the Russian Tea Room's Russian Cream, a Brandied Fruit Compote, or Bananas Flambées. Wines also enhance other fruit desserts — Barbetta Restaurant's Pears Baked in Burgundy, Tipsy Raspberries, or Peaches in Chablis.

A Mixed Melon Ball Compote is a summer treat for which you don't need a recipe; an interesting variation is the Cantaloupe Cocktail, flavored with lemon and lime and garnished with mint. Other fruit desserts can be baked and served warm — Maurice Moore-Betty's Plums Grasmere and Richard Sax's remarkable Italian Stuffed Peaches. Honey Apples are a homier, more casual fruit dessert. Other warm apple treats are Pennsylvania Dutch Apple Dessert (made with oatmeal for a wonderful texture) and Apple Brandy Apples (worthy of a holiday meal).

Also in this section are a selection of sauces — for use on ice cream, to enliven supermarket pound cake, or to enhance many other desserts.

Pies & Pie Crusts

Quick Basic Pie Crust
Almond Crumb Crust
Chocolate Crumb Crust
Graham Cracker Crumb Crust
No-Roll Pie Crust
Quick Company Pie
Sour Cream Blueberry Pie
Cream Cheese Pie
Ten-Minute Chocolate Pie
Easy As Pie
Creamy Coconut Pie
Super Simple Fruit Pie
Kiwi Tart
Angel Pie (Lemon Custard in
    Meringue)

Speedy Lemon Pie
Lemon Soufflé Pie
Key Lime Pie
Mince Apple Pie
Mince Ice Cream Pie
Orange Freezer Pie
Pecan Pie
Pecan Crunch Pie
Kentucky Derby Pie
Rum Cream Pie
Strawberry Tart
Frozen Strawberry Pie

Quick Basic Pie Crust

(1 9-inch pie crust)

- 1¼ cups all-purpose flour
- 6 tablespoons chilled butter, cut up
- 2 tablespoons lard *or* shortening
- ⅛ teaspoon salt
- ¼ teaspoon sugar
- 3 tablespoons cold water

Place all the ingredients except the water in the bowl of a food processor fitted with the steel blade. Process until the bits of butter are the size of peas. With the machine on, add the water gradually through the feed tube until the dough just begins to form a ball. Turn off immediately. This dough may be used without chilling. For a prebaked shell, roll out the dough, fit into a 9-inch pie plate, prick the bottom thoroughly, and chill for 1 hour before baking.

Preheat the oven to 425°.

Bake the shell for 18 to 20 minutes, pushing the dough down gently if it begins to swell during the baking.

Note: If you wish, fill the unbaked crust with dry beans to prevent bubbling while baking, though pricking the bottom thoroughly should do the job.

Almond Crumb Crust

(1 9-inch pie crust)

- 15 pieces of zwieback (3 by 1½ inches)
- ¼ cup unbleached almonds, shelled
- ¼ cup sugar
- ⅓ cup butter, melted
- ¼ teaspoon cinnamon

In a blender or food processor chop the zwieback and almonds into crumbs. Pour the mixture into a large bowl; add the sugar, butter, and cinnamon and stir until moistened. Press the mixture firmly into a buttered 9-inch pie pan. Chill until firm.

Chocolate Crumb Crust

(1 9-inch pie shell)

- 1⅔ cups chocolate wafer crumbs
- 4 tablespoons butter, softened
- ¼ cup sugar

Preheat the oven to 375°.

In a bowl combine all the ingredients. Press evenly against the bottom and sides of a 9-inch pie plate. Bake for 8 to 10 minutes.

Graham Cracker Crumb Crust

(1 9-inch pie crust)

- 1½ cups graham cracker crumbs
- 4 tablespoons sugar
- ⅓ cup butter, melted

Preheat the oven to 375°.

In a bowl combine all the ingredients. Press the mixture firmly into a 9-inch pie plate. Bake for 15 minutes.

Note: To make this crust without baking, increase the butter to ½ cup. Chill thoroughly before filling.

No-Roll Pie Crust

(1 9-inch pie crust)

- 1½ cups flour
- 1½ teaspoons sugar
- 1 teaspoon salt
- ½ cup vegetable oil
- 2 tablespoons milk

Preheat the oven to 425°.

Sift the dry ingredients into a 9-inch pie plate. In a cup combine the oil and the milk, whip with a fork, and pour at once over the flour mixture. Mix with a fork until moistened. Press evenly and firmly into the bottom and up the sides of the plate. Adjust to a uniform thickness. Bake for 12 to 15 minutes, until lightly golden. Cool and fill as desired.

Quick Company Pie

(6 servings)

- ½ cup raisins
- ½ cup nuts, chopped
- 1 tablespoon vinegar
- ½ cup butter, softened
- ¾ cup sugar
- 2 eggs
- 1 teaspoon cinnamon
- ¼ teaspoon nutmeg
- 1 9-inch unbaked pie shell
- Heavy cream (optional)

Preheat the oven to 400°.

In a small bowl marinate the raisins and nuts in the vinegar. Combine the butter, sugar, eggs, cinnamon, and nutmeg in a bowl and beat well. Add the marinated fruit. Spoon the mixture into the pie shell. Bake for 30 to 35 minutes. Serve with cream, if you wish.

Sour Cream Blueberry Pie

(8 servings)

    1 pint blueberries, washed and dried
    1 9-inch baked graham cracker crust
    1 6-ounce jar red currant jelly, melted
    1 cup sour cream

Place the berries in the crust and pour the jelly evenly over them. Cover with a thin layer of the sour cream. Chill in the refrigerator for 1 hour.

Cream Cheese Pie

(8 servings)

    1 8-ounce package cream cheese, softened
    2 eggs
    ¾ cup sugar
    2 teaspoons vanilla
    1 9-inch baked graham cracker crust
    1½ cups sour cream
    3 tablespoons sugar
    1 teaspoon vanilla

Preheat the oven to 350°.

In a bowl combine the cream cheese, eggs, sugar, and the 2 teaspoons vanilla and beat well. Pour the mixture into the crust. Bake for 20 to 25 minutes. Cool for about 5 minutes. Mix the sour cream, sugar, and additional vanilla in a bowl and spread the mixture over the pie. Bake for 5 more minutes. Chill.

Variation: A topping of thawed and drained frozen berries or cherries would be an excellent complement for this pie.

Ten-Minute Chocolate Pie

(8 servings)

    4 ounces German's Sweet Chocolate
    ⅓ cup milk
    2 tablespoons sugar
    1 3-ounce package cream cheese, softened
    8 ounces frozen whipped topping, thawed
    1 9-inch unbaked graham cracker *or* chocolate crumb crust
    Chocolate shavings (garnish)

In a saucepan heat the chocolate and 2 tablespoons of the milk over low heat, stirring constantly. In a bowl beat the sugar into the cheese, then add the remaining milk and the chocolate mixture. Beat until smooth. Fold in the thawed topping. Spoon into the crust and freeze for at least 4 hours. Garnish with chocolate shavings and serve.

Easy As Pie

(6–8 servings)

    ¾ cup sugar
    4 eggs
    2 cups milk
    1 cup shredded coconut
    ½ cup buttermilk biscuit mix
    ½ stick butter
    1 teaspoon vanilla
    Whipped cream, flavored with liqueur
      (Kahlua, Creme de Cacao, Grand
      Marnier) (optional)

Preheat the oven to 350°.

Butter a 9-inch glass pie plate. Put all the ingredients (except the cream) into a blender and blend for 2 minutes. Pour the mixture into the pie plate and bake for 1 hour or until browned. Serve with the flavored whipped cream.

Creamy Coconut Pie

(8 servings)

    2   tablespoons soft butter
    2½ cups moist shredded coconut
    3   eggs
    1   tablespoon lemon juice
    ¾   cup sugar
    12 ounces cream cheese, cut up to
        facilitate blending
    Sweetened whipped cream (optional)

Spread the butter thickly and smoothly over the bottom and sides of a 9-inch pie pan. Sprinkle 1½ cups of the coconut over the pan and pat firmly into the butter. Chill.

Preheat the oven to 350°.

Put the eggs, juice, sugar, and cheese into the container of a food processor or blender and whip until smooth. Add the remaining cup of coconut and blend at low speed until it is finely grated. Pour the mixture into the prepared shell and bake for 25 minutes or until set. Cool. Top with whipped cream if you like.

Super Simple Fruit Pie

(6–8 servings)

2 8-ounce containers of fruit yogurt
1 9-ounce container of frozen whipped topping, thawed
1 9-inch baked graham cracker crust
Cut fruit or whole berries (garnish)
Graham cracker crumbs (garnish)
Whipped topping (garnish)

In a bowl blend the yogurt and thawed topping, using a wire whisk. Pour into the pie shell and chill for several hours or overnight. Garnish as desired with fruit, crumbs, or whipped topping.

Kiwi Tart

(4 servings)

1 sheet pre-rolled puff pastry, 9 by 10 inches (frozen)
1 egg yolk mixed with 1 tablespoon water
¾ cup milk
1 tablespoon cornstarch
2 tablespoons sugar
1 egg yolk, slightly beaten
¼ cup heavy cream
½ pint strawberries, washed, hulled, and halved lengthwise
Small bunch green grapes, well washed
1 kiwi, peeled, sliced, each slice cut in half
¼ cup apple jelly
1 tablespoon water

Preheat the oven to 450°.

Thaw the pastry as directed and cut it in half lengthwise. Place one half on a cookie sheet and brush with the egg yolk and water mixture. On the other half mark a line 1 inch from each side. With a sharp knife, cut out the center rectangle, leaving the 1-inch "frame." Place the frame on the other half, lining up the sides evenly. With a very sharp knife, gently score the frame with large X's. Brush with the egg yolk. Bake for 15 minutes, until the pastry is puffed and golden. From the remaining pastry, cut 4 large leaves and 2 flower shapes. Brush with the egg yolk and bake for 10 to 15 minutes.

Combine the milk, cornstarch, and sugar in a small saucepan and slowly heat to the boiling point, stirring constantly. When thickened, remove from the heat and spoon a little of the mixture into the beaten egg yolk. Stir the egg into the milk mixture in the saucepan and heat just until the mixture starts to boil. Pour into a small bowl and re-frigerate, covered with plastic wrap placed directly on the custard. Whip the heavy cream until stiff, then fold into the custard.

Pour the custard into the pastry shell and arrange the strawberries, grapes, and kiwi on top. Melt the jelly with the water in a small saucepan over low heat. Brush the fruit with the melted jelly. Serve.

Angel Pie
(Lemon Custard in Meringue)

(6 servings)

3 egg whites
¼ teaspoon cream of tartar
1 cup sugar
4 egg yolks
½ cup sugar
Juice and rind of 1 large lemon, grated
1 cup heavy cream, stiffly beaten

Preheat the oven to 300°.

Line a 9-inch layer cake pan with parchment paper. In a bowl beat the egg whites until foamy. Sprinkle with the cream of tartar. Beat in the sugar gradually. Spread meringue into the pan and up the sides. Bake for 1 hour. Turn off the heat and cool in the oven.

In the top of a double boiler over hot water, beat the egg yolks and sugar until thick and lemon-colored, adding the lemon juice and rind (about 6 minutes). Cool.

Spread the meringue with half the whipped cream, then spread on the lemon custard. Top with the rest of the cream. Cover with plastic wrap and refrigerate overnight.

Speedy Lemon Pie

(6–8 servings)

- 1 quart vanilla ice cream, softened
- 1 6-ounce can frozen lemonade concentrate, thawed
- 1 9-inch baked pie shell or crumb crust
- Grated lemon rind (garnish)
- Whipped cream (garnish)

In a food processor combine the ice cream and lemonade until smooth. Pour into the pie shell. Freeze until firm, about 2 hours. Let stand at room temperature for 10 minutes before serving. Garnish with the grated lemon rind and whipped cream.

Lemon Soufflé Pie

(8 servings)

- 1 tablespoon unflavored gelatin
- ¼ cup water
- 2 eggs
- ¾ cup sugar
- Rind of ½ lemon, grated
- Juice of ½ lemon
- 1¼ cups heavy cream, whipped
- 1 baked 9-inch pie shell
- Fresh strawberries (optional)
- Candied violets (optional)

In a metal measuring cup soften the gelatin in the water. Place the cup in a pan of simmering water until the gelatin dissolves. In a bowl beat the eggs with the sugar until light yellow. Stir in the lemon juice, rind, and the gelatin. Let thicken slightly. Fold the cream into the custard and pour into the pie shell. Refrigerate for at least 3 hours. Garnish with the strawberries or candied violets if you like.

Key Lime Pie

(8 servings)

1 14-ounce can sweetened condensed milk
4 egg yolks
Juice of 4 limes
Grated zest of 4 limes
2–3 drops green food coloring (optional)
4 egg whites, beaten stiff but not dry
1 unbaked graham cracker crust
½ cup heavy cream, whipped, for garnish

Preheat the oven to 350°.

In a bowl, combine the condensed milk, egg yolks, lime juice, and zest. Mix well, adding the food coloring if desired. Fold in the egg whites. Pour the mixture into the pie shell and bake for 40 minutes. Chill until firm. Decorate with the whipped cream before serving.

Mince Apple Pie

(8 servings)

¾ cup brown sugar
⅓ cup flour
1 unbaked 10-inch pie shell
5 cups pared, sliced apples
2 cups mincemeat
2 tablespoons dark rum or bourbon
8 ¼-inch-thick apple rings, pared and cored
2 tablespoons butter, cut up

Preheat the oven to 425°.

In a bowl combine the sugar and flour and sprinkle ¼ cup of the mixture into the shell. Layer the apple slices and the sugar mixture, reserving ¼ cup of the sugar mixture. Combine the mincemeat and liquor and spread over the apples. Press the apple rings into the top. Sprinkle the reserved sugar mixture on top and dot with the butter. Bake for 40 minutes.

Mince Ice Cream Pie

(6–8 servings)

8–12 ounces prepared mincemeat, as desired
1 quart vanilla ice cream, softened
2 tablespoons dark rum
1 9-inch baked pie shell or graham cracker crust
½ cup cream, whipped

In a bowl combine the mincemeat, ice cream and rum, and pour into the crust. Freeze. Top with the whipped cream before serving.

Orange Freezer Pie

(8 servings)

Crust:
1 cup finely crushed graham crackers
¼ cup sugar
2 teaspoons cinnamon
¼ teaspoon nutmeg
1½ tablespoons melted butter
1 egg white

1 quart vanilla ice cream, softened
1 6-ounce can frozen orange juice concentrate, thawed
2 tablespoons Grand Marnier
Rind of 1 orange, grated

To make the crust, preheat the oven to 350°.

In a bowl combine the crumbs with the remaining ingredients and blend well. Press the mixture into a buttered 9-inch pie plate. Bake for 5 to 8 minutes. Cool.

In a bowl combine the ice cream with the orange juice and Grand Marnier. Stir until smooth. Pour the mixture into the crust and sprinkle the orange rind over the top. Freeze for at least 6 hours. For easier cutting, let the pie soften in the refrigerator for 30 minutes before serving.

Pecan Pie

(8 servings)

3 eggs
1 cup dark corn syrup
½ cup sugar
½ teaspoon vanilla
1 tablespoon butter
1 cup pecans
1 unbaked 9-inch pie shell

Preheat the oven to 375°.

In a bowl combine the first 6 ingredients. Pour into the pie shell. Bake for 10 minutes. Reduce the heat to 350° and continue baking until the pie is just firm in the middle (about 35 to 40 minutes). Serve warm or at room temperature.

Pecan Crunch Pie

(6–8 servings)

1 teaspoon vanilla
½ teaspoon baking powder
3 egg whites, beaten stiff
1 cup pecans
1 cup sugar
¾ cup Ritz crackers, finely crumbled
Whipped cream (garnish)

Preheat the oven to 325°.

Sprinkle the vanilla and the baking powder over the beaten egg whites. Slowly fold in the pecans, sugar, and the crackers. Bake in a buttered 9-inch pie pan for 40 minutes. Top with the whipped cream.

Note: This pie is tastier if made a day in advance.

Kentucky Derby Pie

(6–8 servings)

- 1 9-inch pie shell, baked for 15 minutes and cooled
- ½ cup butter
- ¾ cup sugar
- ½ cup flour
- 2 eggs
- 1 cup semisweet chocolate bits
- 1 cup pecans
- 2½ tablespoons bourbon
- Sweetened whipped cream (garnish)

Preheat the oven to 350°.

In the bowl of a food processor blend the butter, sugar, flour, and eggs until smooth. Add the chocolate, nuts, and bourbon and process for 3 seconds. Pour into the cooled pie shell and bake for 30 to 35 minutes. Serve at room temperature garnished with whipped cream.

Rum Cream Pie

(8 servings)

- 1 tablespoon unflavored gelatin
- ¼ cup dark rum
- 2 eggs, separated
- ⅔ cup sweetened condensed milk
- ⅛ teaspoon salt
- ½ teaspoon vanilla
- ¼ cup boiling water
- 1 9-inch baked graham cracker crust
- Semisweet chocolate (garnish)
- ½ cup heavy cream, whipped (garnish)

In a small bowl soften the gelatin in the rum. In another bowl beat the egg yolks until light. Stir in the milk, salt, and vanilla. Pour the boiling water over the gelatin to dissolve it and stir it into the egg yolk mixture. Beat the egg whites until stiff but not too dry. Fold into the egg yolk mixture. Pour into the crust. Refrigerate until set, at least 3 hours. Before serving, grate the chocolate over the top and pipe the whipped cream around the edge.

Strawberry Tart

(6 servings)

1 package instant vanilla pudding mix
2 cups half-and-half
2 tablespoons Cointreau
1 cup heavy cream, whipped
1 baked 9-inch pie shell
1 quart strawberries, washed and hulled
1 cup currant jelly
4 tablespoons hot water

In a bowl prepare the pudding according to the package directions, substituting the half-and-half for the milk. Add the Cointreau. Combine the whipped cream with pudding and pour into the crust. Arrange the strawberries on top. In a saucepan melt the jelly with the hot water over low heat and brush over the berries to form a glaze.

Frozen Strawberry Pie

(8 servings)

1 10-ounce package frozen strawberries, thawed and drained
1 egg white
½ cup sugar
2 teaspoons lemon juice
1 tablespoon Grand Marnier
½ cup heavy cream, whipped
1 baked 9-inch pie shell or crumb crust

In a bowl beat the berries, egg white, sugar, lemon juice, and Grand Marnier with an electric mixer until thick and creamy, about 5 to 7 minutes. Fold the whipped cream into the mixture and spoon into the pie shell. Freeze for at least 6 hours or overnight.

Cakes & Frostings

Crazy Cupcakes
Wacky Cake
Danish Apple Cake
Carrot Cake from the Morning Glory
  Café
Blueberry Blender Cake
Sinfully Rich Cheesecake
Blueberry-Pineapple Cheesecake
Chocolate Cheesecake
Wolfgang Puck's Chocolate Cake
  (*Gâteau au Chocolat*)
Sallie Y. Williams's Mocha Cake

Quick Mocha Chocolate Cake
Ann Cashion's Mississippi Mud Cake
Poppy Seed Cake
Raspberry Ladyfinger Cake
Orange Sponge Cake
Orange Frosting
Cream Cheese Frosting
Confectioners' Sugar Icing
Mocha Frosting
Quick Chocolate Frosting
Chocolate Butter Cream Frosting

Crazy Cupcakes

(1 dozen)

1 cup sugar
1 egg
½ cup milk
½ cup cocoa
½ cup shortening
1½ cups cake flour
¼ teaspoon salt
1 teaspoon baking powder
½ teaspoon baking soda
½ cup boiling water
1 teaspoon vanilla

Preheat the oven to 325°.

In a bowl beat all the ingredients together for 3 minutes. Pour the batter into paper cups in muffin pans and bake for 30 minutes. Cool; then frost as desired.

Wacky Cake

(6–8 servings)

1 cup sugar
1 teaspoon baking soda
3 tablespoons cocoa
1½ cups flour
½ teaspoon salt
6 tablespoons vegetable oil
1 tablespoon vinegar
1 teaspoon vanilla
1 cup water

Preheat the oven to 375°.

Sift the dry ingredients into a well-greased 8-inch-square pan. Make 3 holes. Add the oil to one, the vinegar and vanilla to the others. Pour the water over all and mix well with a wooden spoon. Bake for 25 minutes. Cool and cut into squares.

Danish Apple Cake

(6–8 servings)

½ cup butter
2 cups dry white bread crumbs
1 tablespoon sugar
1¼ teaspoons almond extract
2 cups sweetened applesauce
¼ cup raspberry *or* currant jelly
½ cup heavy cream
1 tablespoon confectioners' sugar

Melt the butter. In a bowl toss the crumbs and sugar with the butter until golden. Stir in 1 teaspoon of the almond extract. Butter a 1-quart casserole. Alternate layers of the crumbs and the applesauce in the casserole, beginning and ending with the crumbs. Cover and chill for 1 hour. Invert onto a serving plate and unmold. Melt the jelly over low heat and spread over the cake. Beat the cream until stiff, stirring in the remaining ¼ teaspoon almond extract and the confectioners' sugar. Decorate the cake with the cream.

Carrot Cake from the Morning Glory Café

(8–10 servings)

2 cups flour
2 cups sugar
1 teaspoon salt
1 teaspoon nutmeg
2 teaspoons cinnamon
2 teaspoons baking powder
2 teaspoons baking soda
4 eggs, beaten
1½ cups vegetable oil
3 cups grated raw carrot
1 cup chopped pecans *or* walnuts
¾ cup whole pecans *or* walnuts (garnish)

Frosting (1½ cups):
½ cup butter, softened
8 ounces cream cheese, softened
1 16-ounce box confectioners' sugar
2 teaspoons vanilla

Preheat the oven to 325°.

Combine the dry ingredients in a bowl and add the eggs and oil. Fold in the carrots and nuts. Bake immediately in a well-greased 10-inch tube pan for 45 minutes or until a toothpick comes out clean.

To make the frosting, blend the butter with the cheese, slowly adding the sugar and vanilla. Frost the cake when cool and decorate with the whole nuts.

Variation: Add 1 apple, peeled and grated, and reduce the amount of grated carrots to 2⅔ cups.

Blueberry Blender Cake

(6 servings)

1½	cups milk
4	eggs
½	cup flour
¼	cup sugar
2	teaspoons vanilla
2	cups fresh *or* dry-frozen blueberries

Confectioners' sugar

Preheat the oven to 350°. Generously butter a 6-cup rectangular baking dish or 10-inch pie pan.

In a food processor or blender combine the milk, eggs, flour, sugar, and vanilla and mix for 30 seconds, stopping to scrape down the sides as necessary. Spread the berries in the baking dish and pour the batter evenly over them. Bake for about 1¼ hours or until the top is browned. Dust with the confectioners' sugar and serve warm.

Sinfully Rich Cheesecake

(8–10 servings)

Crust:

1⅓	cups graham cracker crumbs (¼ pound)
5	tablespoons sugar
1½	teaspoons cinnamon
½	teaspoon allspice
6	tablespoons melted butter
3	8-ounce packages cream cheese, softened
1	cup sugar
3	eggs
1	teaspoon vanilla
1	cup sour cream
3	tablespoons sugar

Preheat the oven to 375°. Butter an 8-inch springform pan.

In a bowl blend the crust ingredients and line the prepared pan with the mixture.

Blend the cream cheese with the 1 cup sugar and beat until fluffy. Beat in the eggs and ½ teaspoon of the vanilla. Pour the filling mixture into the pan and bake for 25 minutes. Remove from the oven and turn the oven up to 500°. Whip the sour cream lightly and add the 3 tablespoons sugar and the remaining ½ teaspoon vanilla. Pour over the cake and bake for 5 minutes. Cool at room temperature and chill until firm, about 3 hours.

Blueberry-Pineapple Cheesecake

(8–10 servings)

- 1 cup graham cracker crumbs
- 2 tablespoons sugar
- 2 tablespoons butter or margarine, melted
- 3 8-ounce packages cream cheese, at room temperature
- 1 cup sugar
- 2 tablespoons flour
- 1 tablespoon grated lemon rind
- 2 tablespoons lemon juice
- ½ teaspoon vanilla
- 5 eggs
- 1 cup heavy cream
- ¼ cup pineapple preserves
- 1 cup crushed pineapple, drained
- ¼ cup blueberry jam
- 1 pint blueberries

Mix the graham cracker crumbs, the 2 tablespoons sugar, and the melted butter together in a small bowl. Press the mixture into the bottom of a 9-inch springform pan and refrigerate.

Preheat the oven to 350°.

In a large bowl beat the cream cheese, the 1 cup sugar, the flour, and the lemon rind until smooth. Beat in the lemon juice, vanilla extract, and the eggs. Add the heavy cream and beat until well blended. Pour into the prepared pan and bake for 50 minutes or until almost firm. Remove to a wire rack. Carefully run the tip of a sharp knife around the edge of the cake. Cool completely, then refrigerate for 4 hours or overnight, lightly covered.

In a small saucepan, melt the pineapple preserves. Add the crushed pineapple and cool the mixture. Melt the blueberry preserves in another small saucepan. Add the blueberries and cool. Remove the side of the springform pan. Using a toothpick, mark the top of the cake into 8 wedges. Spoon the pineapple and blueberry toppings onto alternating sections.

Chocolate Cheesecake

(16 servings)

1 recipe Graham Cracker Crumb Crust
1 6-ounce package semisweet chocolate bits, melted
3 8-ounce packages cream cheese, cut up
1 cup sugar
2 eggs
2 teaspoons cocoa
1 teaspoon vanilla
1½ cups sour cream
Sweetened cocoa powder (optional)

Preheat the oven to 350°. Line a 9-inch springform pan with the graham cracker crust mixture.

In the bowl of a food processor combine all the ingredients except the sour cream and cocoa powder and blend. Remove to a bowl and stir in the sour cream. Pour into the crust and bake for 45 minutes. Cool in the pan for 1 hour, then refrigerate overnight. Before serving, sift the cocoa powder over top of cake if you wish.

Wolfgang Puck's Chocolate Cake
(Gâteau au Chocolat)

(1 10-inch cake)

8 ounces bittersweet chocolate, cut into small pieces
4 ounces unsalted butter, cut into small pieces
5 eggs, separated
Pinch of salt
⅔ cup sugar
Confectioners' sugar
Unsweetened whipped cream (optional)

Preheat the oven to 325°. Butter and flour a 10-inch round cake pan.

Combine the chocolate and butter and melt over simmering water. Whisk together the egg yolks, salt, and all but 3 tablespoons of the sugar. Stir the melted chocolate into the egg yolks until thoroughly combined. With an electric mixer on medium speed, beat the egg whites until soft peaks form. Gradually beat in the remaining sugar and beat until the egg whites are stiff but not dry.

Carefully fold the chocolate mixture into the egg whites. Pour into the prepared pan. Bake for 1¼ hours. Turn out onto a rack immediately. As the cake cools, the center will sink and crack — do not worry.

Dust the cake with powdered sugar and serve with unsweetened whipped cream.

Sallie Y. Williams's Mocha Cake

(6–8 servings)

- ½ cup sugar
- 3 eggs
- ¾ cup sifted cake flour
- 1 tablespoon melted butter
- 1 recipe Mocha Butter Cream Frosting (*see below*)
- ½ cup chopped pecans *or* walnuts
- ½ cup whole pecan *or* walnut halves

Preheat the oven to 425°. Generously butter and flour a 9-inch cake pan.

Beat the sugar and the eggs in a metal mixing bowl until just combined. Set the bowl over hot but not boiling water and beat with an electric mixer until the mixture is light yellow and has increased at least three times in volume (about 6–8 minutes). When the batter is ready, it will fall in sheets or ribbons from the beaters.

Remove the bowl from the hot water and gently fold in the flour (do not stir or beat). Mix the flour in thoroughly, then fold in the melted butter. Pour into the prepared cake pan.

Bake for about 20 minutes or until the center springs back when touched and the cake has begun to pull away from the sides of the pan. Let the cake cool for 5 minutes; turn it out onto a rack covered with waxed paper and cool completely.

Using a serrated knife, split the cake horizontally into two layers. (The cake will not be tall, but it is very rich.) Place the bottom layer on a round of cardboard the same diameter as the cake. Cover the first layer with a thin layer of the frosting and top with the second cake layer. Spread a thin layer of the frosting over the top and sides of the cake. Sprinkle the top with the chopped nuts and press the nut halves into the frosting around the base of the cake.

Mocha Butter Cream Frosting (2 cups):
- 2 cups sugar
- ½ cup water
- 4 egg yolks, beaten
- 3 tablespoons strong coffee
- 1 cup butter, softened

Melt the sugar in the water in a heavy saucepan. Cover and cook for 10 minutes. Uncover and continue to boil until the syrup reaches 235° (the "soft ball" stage) on a candy thermometer (15 to 30 minutes or longer depending on the temperature and humidity). Cool slightly.

Slowly beat the cooled syrup into the egg yolks, whisking constantly. Whisk or beat with an electric mixer until the mixture is light and creamy, about 5 minutes. Add the coffee and butter and blend to the consistency you want.

Sallie Y. Williams's Mocha Cake

Quick Mocha Chocolate Cake

(8 servings)

2 ounces unsweetened chocolate
1 egg
1 cup sugar
⅓ cup vegetable oil
1 teaspoon vanilla
¾ cup strong coffee
1⅓ cups flour
1 teaspoon baking soda
1 teaspoon baking powder

Preheat the oven to 350°. Butter and flour an 8-inch round cake pan.

Melt the chocolate in the top of a double boiler. In a bowl beat the egg and slowly add the sugar, beating until well blended. Beat in the oil, vanilla, melted chocolate, and coffee. Sift the flour, baking soda, and baking powder together and add to the other ingredients, beating vigorously until smooth. Pour into the prepared cake pan and bake for 35 to 40 minutes. When cool, frost as desired.

Ann Cashion's Mississippi Mud Cake

(12 servings)

½ pound semisweet chocolate
½ pound butter
5 eggs, separated
1⅓ cups sugar
¼ cup bourbon
1½ cups sifted cake flour
1 cup chopped pecans
3 cups miniature marshmallows

Icing:
½ pound semisweet chocolate
3 tablespoons butter
⅓ cup heavy cream

Preheat the oven to 350°.

In a double boiler or over very low heat, melt the chocolate and the butter. Beat the egg whites with half of the sugar until they form peaks but are not yet stiff. Set aside. Beat the egg yolks with the remaining sugar until the mixture is pale yellow. Add the chocolate mixture and the bourbon to the egg yolk mixture, then add the flour and the nuts. Carefully fold in the egg whites. Turn the batter into an 8- by 11-inch buttered and floured pan and bake for 25 minutes. Remove the cake from the oven, distribute the marshmallows over the surface, return to the oven, and bake until the marshmallows have melted and browned. Cool the cake in the pan.

To prepare the icing, in a double boiler or over very low heat melt the chocolate and butter with the cream. Pour the mixture through a sieve onto the surface of the cooled cake. Spread the frosting evenly over the cake and let it set.

Poppy Seed Cake

(2 loaves or 1 kugelhopf mold)

1½	cups vegetable oil
2	cups sugar
1	cup milk
4	eggs
3	cups flour
3	teaspoons baking powder
1	teaspoon salt
1	teaspoon vanilla
¾	cup poppy seeds

Preheat the oven to 350°.

Combine the ingredients in the order listed. Pour into 2 loaf pans or a kugelhopf mold and bake for 1 hour.

Raspberry Ladyfinger Cake

(6 servings)

3	packages frozen raspberries, thawed and drained (reserve juice)
½	cup kirsch
½	cup sugar
2	3-ounce packages ladyfingers, split lengthwise
Whipped cream (optional)	

Marinate the raspberries in the kirsch and sugar for several hours, stirring occasionally. Strain the berries, reserving the juice, and purée them in a food mill. Dip the ladyfingers into the juice and press into the sides and bottom of a 5- to 6-cup soufflé dish. Add one third of the berries to the bottom of the mold and cover with additional moistened ladyfingers. Repeat twice, ending with a layer of ladyfingers. Cover with plastic wrap and top with a plate. Place a weight on the plate and refrigerate for at least 4 hours. Unmold and serve cold, surrounded by the juice. Serve with whipped cream if desired.

Orange Sponge Cake

(4 servings)

1 cup sifted all-purpose flour
1 teaspoon baking powder
¼ teaspoon salt
3 eggs
1 cup sugar
1 tablespoon grated orange peel
⅓ cup fresh orange juice
1 recipe Orange Frosting
Kumquats (garnish)

Preheat the oven to 350°.

Sift the flour, baking powder, and salt together and set aside. In a medium-size bowl, beat the eggs until thick and lemon colored. With an electric portable mixer, beat in the sugar a little at a time, then continue beating for an additional 3 to 5 minutes. (The mixture should be very thick.) At low speed, beat in the flour mixture just until smooth. Add the orange peel and juice and beat until just combined.

Pour into an ungreased 8-inch tube pan and bake for 45 minutes or until a cake tester comes out clean. Place the pan over the neck of a bottle and allow it to cool completely before removing the cake from the pan. Frost with Orange Frosting and garnish with kumquats.

Orange Frosting

(Enough for an 8-inch tube cake)

3 tablespoons butter *or* margarine, softened
1 egg yolk
1 tablespoon grated orange peel
3 cups sifted confectioners' sugar
2 tablespoons fresh orange juice (or more)

Beat the butter in a medium-size bowl until light and fluffy. Add the egg yolk and orange peel and beat to combine. Beat in the confectioners' sugar 1 cup at a time, alternating with tablespoons of the orange juice. Beat until light and fluffy. If the frosting is too stiff, beat in a little more orange juice.

Cream Cheese Frosting

(Enough for a 2-layer cake)

- ¼ pound unsalted butter
- 1 16-ounce box confectioners' sugar
- 1 8-ounce package cream cheese, softened
- 2 teaspoons vanilla

In a bowl combine all the ingredients and beat until the mixture is light and creamy and of spreading consistency.

Confectioners' Sugar Icing

(Enough for 1 dozen cupcakes)

- 2 cups confectioners' sugar
- 1 teaspoon vanilla
- Heavy cream

Sift the sugar into a mixing bowl and add the vanilla. Beat in the cream until mixture is a good consistency for spreading.

Note: This icing can be tinted with food coloring. You can tint the whole mixture one color or separate it into smaller bowls and tint each portion a different color.

Mocha Frosting

(Enough for a 2-layer cake)

- 6 tablespoons unsweetened cocoa
- 6 tablespoons hot strong coffee
- 6 tablespoons butter, softened
- 1 teaspoon vanilla
- 3 cups confectioners' sugar

In a bowl combine the cocoa and coffee. Beat in the butter and vanilla gradually, adding the sugar until the frosting is the desired consistency for spreading.

Quick Chocolate Frosting

(2 cups)

- 4 ounces semisweet chocolate
- ¼ cup butter
- 3 cups confectioners' sugar, sifted
- 1 teaspoon vanilla
- ⅓ cup milk

In a saucepan melt the chocolate with the butter over low heat. Remove from the heat. Add the sugar, vanilla, and milk and beat to the desired consistency for spreading. The frosting will thicken as it cools, and additional milk may be needed to thin it.

Note: This amount will frost the top and sides of a 2-layer cake or 24 cupcakes.

Chocolate Butter Cream Frosting

(2 cups)

¼   cup cocoa
2⅔   cups confectioners' sugar
6   tablespoons butter
4–5 tablespoons milk
1   teaspoon vanilla

In a bowl combine the cocoa and confectioners' sugar. In another bowl cream the butter with ½ cup of the cocoa mixture. Add the remaining mixture, alternating with the milk. Blend in the vanilla and beat to the desired consistency for spreading.

Note: This classic frosting is excellent for cupcakes, sheet cakes, or layer cakes of all varieties, especially yellow or white cakes.

Variation: For a darker frosting, use ¾ cup cocoa.

Cookies

Apricot Bars
No-Bake Brownies
Chocolate Drops
Meringues
Macaroons
Graham Cracker Thins
Overnight Kisses
Orange Marmalade Drop Cakes
Walnut Bars
Pecan Crisps
Nutty Rum Balls
Peanut Butter Cookies

Apricot Bars

(20–24 cookies)

⅔ cup dried apricots
½ cup butter
¼ cup sugar
1⅓ cups flour, sifted
2 eggs
1 cup brown sugar
½ teaspoon baking powder
¼ teaspoon salt
½ teaspoon vanilla
½ cup walnut pieces
Confectioners' sugar

Rinse the apricots, place them in a small saucepan with water to cover, bring to a boil, and cook over medium-low heat for 10 minutes. Drain the apricots, let cool, chop, and set aside.

Preheat the oven to 350°. Grease a 9-by-9-inch cake pan.

In a bowl combine the butter, sugar, and 1 cup of the flour until crumbly. Pack the mixture into the greased pan and bake for 20 minutes.

While this layer is baking, beat the eggs well and add the brown sugar. Sift together the remaining ⅓ cup flour, the baking powder, and the salt, then combine well with the egg mixture. Add the vanilla, nuts, and apricots. Spread this mixture over the baked layer and bake for 25 minutes more. Cool in the pan, cut into squares, and dust with the confectioners' sugar.

No-Bake Brownies

(16 squares)

1 12-ounce package semisweet chocolate bits
¼ cup butter
2½ cups graham cracker crumbs
1 cup walnuts, chopped
1 14-ounce can condensed milk
1 teaspoon vanilla

In the top of a double boiler melt the chocolate with the butter and stir until smooth. Combine the remaining ingredients in a bowl, then stir in the chocolate mixture. (The batter will be very thick.) Pat the batter evenly into an 8- or 9-inch-square baking pan. Let stand at room temperature for several hours; cut into squares. Store at room temperature.

Chocolate Drops

(48 small cookies)

- 2½ cups all-purpose flour
- 2 teaspoons baking powder
- ½ teaspoon salt
- ½ cup shortening
- 1 cup sugar
- 2 eggs
- 3 ounces unsweetened chocolate, melted
- ½ cup milk
- 1 teaspoon vanilla

Vanilla Glaze:
- 1½ cups confectioners' sugar
- Dash of salt
- ½ teaspoon vanilla extract
- 1–2 tablespoons milk

Preheat the oven to 375°.

Sift the flour, baking powder, and salt together and set aside. Cream the shortening and sugar; beat in the eggs and chocolate. Add the flour mixture and milk alternately, beginning and ending with the flour. Stir in the vanilla. Using a teaspoon, drop onto a lightly greased cookie sheet, 2 inches apart. Bake for 15 minutes or until set. Remove to a wire rack.

To make the glaze, in a medium-size bowl beat all the ingredients together with an electric mixer until smooth. Frost the cookies when they are cool.

Meringues

(3 dozen)

- 6 egg whites
- ½ teaspoon cream of tartar
- 2 cups sugar

Preheat the oven to 275°. Line a baking sheet with parchment paper or brown paper.

Beat the egg whites until foamy. Sprinkle with the cream of tartar. Gradually beat in the sugar and continue beating until stiff and glossy. Drop by teaspoonfuls or pipe in small mounds onto the lined baking sheet: Bake for 1 hour and turn the oven off. Let the meringues dry out until cool or overnight.

Meringue Cups with Ice Cream

Macaroons

(2½ dozen)

    1 cup almond paste
    1 cup confectioners' sugar
Pinch of salt
    1 tablespoon seedless raspberry
       preserves
    ¼ teaspoon vanilla or almond extract
    ¼ cup egg whites (2 or 3)
Sugar

Preheat the oven to 300°. Line a baking sheet with parchment paper.

In a food processor fitted with the steel blade, blend the almond paste, sugar, and salt. Add the preserves and vanilla. Process, adding the whites one at a time, to a thickness suitable for piping. Pipe in 1-inch rounds on the lined baking sheet. Sprinkle with the granulated sugar and bake for 14 to 16 minutes. For easy removal, place the paper with the macaroons on a damp dishtowel spread on a flat surface. The macaroons will lift off easily as they cool. Cool completely and store in an airtight container.

Graham Cracker Thins

(24 cookies)

    12 double graham crackers
    ¼   pound butter
    ¼   pound margarine
    1   cup brown sugar
    1   cup chopped nuts

Preheat the oven to 350°.

Put the crackers in a single layer in a jelly roll pan. In a saucepan mix the butter, margarine, and sugar and bring to a boil. Boil for *only* 2 minutes by the clock and remove from the heat. Stir in the nuts. Pour over the crackers and bake for 10 minutes. Cool slightly; cut while still warm.

Overnight Kisses

(4 dozen)

    2 egg whites
    ⅔ cup sugar
    ¼ teaspoon salt
    1 teaspoon vanilla
    1 cup chocolate chips

Preheat the oven to 350°.

Beat the egg whites until foamy. Gradually add the sugar, salt, and vanilla and beat until stiff. Fold in the chocolate chips. Drop by teaspoonfuls onto an ungreased cookie sheet. Put the baking sheet in the oven and turn it *off* immediately. Leave the cookies in the oven overnight or until the oven is cool.

Orange Marmalade Drop Cakes

(2 dozen)

⅓ cup unsalted butter
⅔ cup sugar
1 egg
6 tablespoons orange marmalade
1½ cups flour
2 teaspoons baking powder

Preheat the oven to 275°.

In a bowl cream together the butter and sugar. Beat the egg, and add it with the marmalade to the butter mixture. Sift together the flour and baking powder and stir into the batter. Drop the batter by teaspoonfuls 2 inches apart onto a greased cookie sheet. Bake for 10 minutes.

Walnut Bars

(24 1½-inch bars)

½ cup butter
½ cup brown sugar
1 cup flour

Topping:
1 cup brown sugar
2 eggs, beaten
Pinch of salt
¼ teaspoon vanilla
2 tablespoons flour
½ teaspoon baking powder
1 cup walnuts, chopped
1½ cups shredded coconut

Preheat the oven to 325°.

In a bowl cream together the butter and the brown sugar. Work in the flour until the mixture is crumbly. Pat the batter smoothly into a shallow pan approximately 7 by 11 inches and bake for 15 minutes.

While the bottom layer is baking, prepare the topping. Combine the brown sugar, eggs, salt, and vanilla. Sift together the flour and baking powder, and combine with the nuts and coconut. Blend the dry ingredients into the egg mixture and pour over the baked layer. Return the pan to the oven and bake for 20–25 minutes more. Cut into bars and remove them from the pan while they are still warm.

Pecan Crisps

(About 3 dozen)

1 egg white, stiffly beaten
1 cup brown sugar
1 teaspoon vanilla
2 cups chopped pecans

Preheat the oven to 350°.

Combine the egg white with the sugar, vanilla, and pecans. Drop by teaspoonfuls onto an ungreased or parchment-covered cookie sheet. Place in the oven, turn it off, and leave the cookies in for 40 minutes.

Nutty Rum Balls

(36 balls)

2 cups finely chopped pecans
2 cups crushed vanilla wafers
2 cups confectioners' sugar
3 tablespoons unsweetened cocoa powder
¼ cup butter, melted
½ teaspoon vanilla
¼ cup dark rum

Combine the pecans, vanilla wafer crumbs, sugar, and cocoa in a large bowl. Stir in the

butter, vanilla, and rum. Shape into 1-inch balls and roll in additional confectioners' sugar, if you wish.

Peanut Butter Cookies

(48 small cookies)

1½ cups all-purpose flour
½ teaspoon baking soda
¼ teaspoon salt
¾ cup chunk-style peanut butter
⅓ cup butter
¼ cup sugar
¼ cup honey
½ teaspoon vanilla extract
1 egg
Semisweet chocolate pieces or chopped peanuts

Sift the flour, baking soda, and salt together and set aside. Beat the peanut butter, butter, and the sugar together until creamy, then beat in the honey, vanilla, and the egg. Gradually stir in the flour mixture.

Preheat the oven to 375°.

Using your hands, roll the dough into ¾-inch balls. Place on a cookie sheet and press with a fork to flatten slightly. Sprinkle each cookie with chocolate pieces or chopped peanuts. Bake for 8 to 10 minutes.

Soufflés & Puddings

Frozen Amaretto Soufflé
Frozen Avocado Soufflé
Chocolate Mousse Chanticleer
Speedy Chocolate Mousse
Another Chocolate Mousse
Easy Chocolate Soufflé
Chocolate Angel Fancy
Chocolate Square
Ginger Mousse
Easy Coffee Mousse
Grand Marnier Mousse
Grasshopper Soufflé
Elizabeth Schneider Colchie's
   Tart Lemon Mousse
Cold Lemon Soufflé
Chilled Strawberry Soufflé
"Double Boiler" Apricot or
   Prune Soufflé
"Double Boiler" Orange Soufflé
"Double Boiler" Praline Soufflé

Caramel Custard
Chilled Apple Cream
Orange Blossom Bowl
Lemon Pudding
Lemon Bread Pudding
Frozen Rum Cream
The Russian Tea Room's
   Russian Cream
Summer Pudding
Elizabeth Esterling's Rice Pudding
Quick Trifle
Zabaglione
Creamy Zabaglione
Extra-Rich Zabaglione
Brown Betty
Apple-Blueberry Crisp
Jean Anderson's Blackberry Cobbler
   with Whole-Wheat Shortbread
   Topping

Frozen Amaretto Soufflé

(4 servings)

- ½ cup macaroons, crumbled
- 1½ tablespoons Amaretto
- 1 pint vanilla ice cream, softened slightly
- ½ cup heavy cream, whipped
- 2 tablespoons toasted almonds, chopped
- 2 teaspoons confectioners' sugar, sifted

Hot Strawberry Sauce

In a bowl stir the macaroon crumbs and the Amaretto into the ice cream. Fold in the whipped cream. Spoon the mixture into a 3-cup metal soufflé dish and freeze overnight. Unmold. Sprinkle the surface with the almonds and sugar. Return to the freezer until ready to serve. Pass the Hot Strawberry Sauce separately.

Frozen Avocado Soufflé

(8 servings)

- ¾ cup sugar
- ¼ cup water
- 8 egg yolks
- 3 ripe avocados, mashed
- 2 ounces Grand Marnier
- 3 egg whites, stiffly beaten
- 2 cups heavy cream, whipped

Sauce Sabayon

In a saucepan, cook the sugar and water for 5 minutes over medium heat. Pour ¾ cup of this syrup into the top of a double boiler and beat with the egg yolks until the mixture is light. Refrigerate. In a bowl, combine the remaining syrup, the avocados, and the liqueur. Fold in the cream, then the egg whites. Pour into individual serving cups or wineglasses and refrigerate. Pass the Sauce Sabayon separately.

Chocolate Mousse Chanticleer

(6 servings)

- ¼ cup butter
- 7 ounces semisweet chocolate
- 5 tablespoons sugar
- 6 eggs, separated

Melt the butter and chocolate in the top of a double boiler. Add the sugar and mix with a wooden spoon until smooth. Set aside and let cool. Beat the egg whites until stiff. When the chocolate mixture is cool add the egg yolks, one by one, stirring until smooth after each addition. Then add the egg whites, spoonful by spoonful, mixing thoroughly. Pour into individual bowls and refrigerate for at least 4 hours before serving.

Speedy Chocolate Mousse

(6 servings)

- 6 ounces semisweet chocolate bits
- 5 tablespoons boiling water
- 4 egg yolks
- 2 tablespoons dark rum
- 4 egg whites, stiffly beaten

In a blender chop the chocolate pieces for 6 seconds. Scrape down the sides and add the boiling water. Blend for 10 seconds. Add the egg yolks and rum. Blend for 3 more seconds or until smooth. Fold the chocolate mixture into the egg whites. Spoon into individual cups and chill for at least 1 hour before serving.

Another Chocolate Mousse

(6–8 servings)

- 1½ cups half-and-half
- 1½ cups semisweet chocolate bits
- 2 eggs
- Pinch of nutmeg
- 1 tablespoon dark rum or cognac

In a saucepan heat the half-and-half over medium heat until it is very hot. Mix all the other ingredients in a blender. Add the half-and-half, blend thoroughly, and pour into a serving dish or individual bowls. Cover and chill until set, at least 4 hours.

Easy Chocolate Soufflé

(4–6 servings)

1   package chocolate pudding mix
1¼ cups milk
1½ tablespoons Kahlua
4   egg whites, stiffly beaten

Preheat the oven to 325°. Butter the bottom and sides of a 6-cup soufflé dish.

In a saucepan cook the pudding with the milk over medium heat until thickened. Cool slightly, then add the Kahlua. Fold into egg whites and then pour into the soufflé dish. Place the dish in a pan of hot water and bake for 45 minutes. Serve immediately.

Chocolate Angel Fancy

(8 servings)

1   angel cake, homemade or purchased
12 ounces semisweet chocolate bits
2   tablespoons water
3   egg yolks, beaten
1   teaspoon vanilla
1   cup heavy cream
1   tablespoon sugar
3   egg whites, stiffly beaten
Chocolate shavings (garnish)

Tear the angel cake into bite-size pieces and place in an 8-cup soufflé dish. In a saucepan, melt the chocolate with the water over low heat. Blend in the egg yolks and vanilla. Cool. In a bowl whip the cream, adding the sugar gradually. Fold the chocolate into the cream; then fold in the egg whites. Pour over the cake and refrigerate overnight. Serve with extra whipped cream, if desired, and decorate with chocolate shavings.

Note: This dessert can be prepared in advance and frozen. Thaw before serving.

Chocolate Square

(8 servings)

8 ounces semisweet chocolate
¼ cup water
6 eggs, separated
½ pound sweet butter, softened
¼ cup sugar
Whipped cream (optional)
Chopped nuts (optional)

Butter the bottom and sides of an 8-inch-square pan. In a saucepan melt the chocolate with the water over medium-low heat. Stir in the egg yolks one at a time. Remove from the heat and add the butter by tablespoons, stirring quickly. In a bowl beat the egg whites to soft peaks and add the sugar gradually. Gently fold in the chocolate mixture. Pour into the buttered pan and chill for 8 hours or overnight. To serve, unmold and decorate, if desired, with the whipped cream and nuts.

Ginger Mousse

(8 servings)

1 tablespoon unflavored gelatin
¼ cup cold water
5 egg yolks
¾ cup sugar
1½ cups milk, scalded
1 cup preserved ginger, minced
½ cup light rum
4 egg whites
Chocolate shavings (garnish)

In a small bowl soften the gelatin in the water. In a saucepan beat the egg yolks with ½ cup of the sugar until the mixture is light. Add the hot milk and cook over low heat until the custard coats a wooden spoon. Do not let it boil. Add the softened gelatin, the ginger, and the rum. Cool.

In a bowl beat the egg whites until foamy. Add the remaining ¼ cup of sugar. Stir one third of the egg whites into the custard; then fold in the remainder. Divide among 8 wineglasses and chill for at least 5 hours. Decorate with chocolate shavings and serve.

Easy Coffee Mousse

(6 servings)

26 marshmallows
1 cup hot, strong coffee
1 cup heavy cream, whipped
½ teaspoon vanilla

In a bowl dissolve the marshmallows in the hot coffee. Let cool; then add the whipped cream and vanilla. Pour into individual glasses and refrigerate. (Do not freeze.)

Grand Marnier Mousse

(8 servings)

2 eggs
¼ cup sugar
1 cup milk, scalded
1 tablespoon unflavored gelatin
¼ cup cold water
3 tablespoons Grand Marnier or more
   to taste
2 cups heavy cream
¾ cup confectioners' sugar
Orange sections *or* candied violets
   (garnish)

In the top of a double boiler beat the eggs with the sugar until the mixture is light. Add the scalded milk and stir over hot water until the mixture coats a wooden spoon. Soften the gelatin in the cold water for 5 minutes; then add to the custard, stirring to dissolve. Add the Grand Marnier. In a bowl whip the cream, adding the confectioners' sugar gradually. Fold the whipped cream into the custard. Chill. Decorate with orange sections or candied violets and serve.

Variation: Transfer the mixture into a bowl or mold lined with ladyfingers and chill.

Grasshopper Soufflé

(8 servings)

2 tablespoons gelatin
2 cups water
1 cup sugar
4 eggs, separated
8 ounces cream cheese, softened
¼ cup Crème de Menthe
1 cup heavy cream, whipped

Make a collar for a 6-cup soufflé dish. In a saucepan soften the gelatin in ½ cup of the water. Add the remaining water and heat gently to dissolve. Beat the egg yolks. Remove the gelatin from the heat and stir in ¾ cup of the sugar and the egg yolks. Return to the heat and simmer for 2 to 3 minutes, stirring all the while. Cool. In a large bowl whip the cream cheese; add the gelatin mixture and the Crème de Menthe. Chill until slightly thickened. Beat the egg whites, adding the remaining ¼ cup sugar. Fold the beaten egg whites and whipped cream into the cheese mixture. Pour into the soufflé dish and chill until firm.

Note: To form a collar, cut a piece of foil or waxed paper 3 inches longer than the circumference of the soufflé dish. Fit it around the top and secure it with a piece of string. It should extend 3 inches above the dish.

Elizabeth Schneider Colchie's Tart Lemon Mousse

(6 servings)

1   envelope unflavored gelatin
¼   cup cold water
2 or 3 large lemons
¾   cup sugar
4   egg whites
Pinch of salt
1   cup heavy cream

Prepare a 4-cup charlotte mold or soufflé dish by pinning or tying a collar of folded waxed paper or aluminum foil around the dish so that it extends 1½ inches above the rim.

In a small saucepan combine the gelatin and cold water and let it stand for 5 minutes. Grate the rind off 2 lemons and squeeze and strain the juice; there should be about 1½ tablespoons rind and ⅔ cup juice. Stir the gelatin mixture over low heat until it dissolves, then add ½ cup of the sugar and continue stirring until the sugar dissolves. Remove the pan from the heat and stir in the lemon peel and lemon juice. Set the saucepan in a bowl of ice water. Stir until the mixture is thick but not set. Remove the bowl from the water and stir vigorously.

Beat the egg whites with the salt until very soft peaks form. Beat in the remaining ¼ cup sugar a tablespoon at a time, beating just until the whites are glossy, but not dry and stiff. Whip the cream just until it mounds gently. Fold the lemon mixture thoroughly into the beaten egg whites, then gently fold in the whipped cream. Spoon the mousse into the prepared mold and chill for at least 4 hours. Before serving, unfasten the collar and peel it away carefully.

Note: Alternatively, the mousse may be chilled in individual crystal glasses or dishes.

Cold Lemon Soufflé

(8 servings)

- 1 tablespoon unflavored gelatin
- ¼ cup cold water
- 3 eggs, separated
- 1 cup sugar
- Juice of 2 lemons
- Rind of 2 lemons, grated
- 2 cups heavy cream
- 2 tablespoon confectioners' sugar
- 1 teaspoon vanilla
- Candied violets (optional)

In a metal measuring cup, soften the gelatin in the cold water. In a bowl beat the egg yolks with the sugar until the mixture is thick and light. Beat in the lemon juice and rind. Beat the egg whites until stiff but not dry. Whip 1½ cups of the cream. Dissolve the gelatin by placing the cup in simmering water. When the gelatin is thoroughly dissolved, fold it into the lemon mixture; then fold in the egg whites, then the whipped cream. Pour the mixture into a 6-cup soufflé dish. Refrigerate until firm and cold. Whip the remaining cream, beating in the confectioners' sugar and vanilla. Garnish the soufflé with rosettes of whipped cream, each topped with a candied violet, if desired.

Chilled Strawberry Soufflé

(8 servings)

- 2 pints strawberries, washed and hulled
- 2 tablespoons unflavored gelatin
- ¾ cup sugar
- ½ cup water
- 1½ tablespoons lemon juice
- 2 tablespoons kirsch
- 3 egg whites
- 1 cup heavy cream, stiffly beaten

Make an oiled aluminum foil collar for a 4-cup soufflé dish. Reserve 8 of the most attractive berries to use as a garnish. Purée the remaining berries in a food processor. If you wish, put the purée through a sieve to remove the seeds. In a saucepan mix the gelatin and ½ cup of the sugar with the water and place over low heat to dissolve. Add the gelatin, juice, and the kirsch to the berries. Refrigerate the mixture until it thickens slightly (about 30 minutes). Beat the egg whites until foamy. Gradually add the remaining ¼ cup sugar and beat until stiff. Fold the beaten egg whites into the strawberries. Fold in the whipped cream. Pour into the soufflé dish and refrigerate until firm, about 4 hours. Garnish with the reserved strawberries.

"Double Boiler" Apricot or Prune Soufflé

(6 servings)

6 egg whites
¼ cup granulated sugar
1 cup cooked apricots or prunes, puréed
Whipped cream (garnish)
Toasted almonds (garnish)

Butter the top pan and the lid of a 2½-quart double boiler and coat both with granulated sugar.

In a bowl beat the egg whites until foamy, adding the sugar until stiff. With a wire whisk, gradually fold in the puréed fruit. Turn the mixture into the prepared double boiler and cover with the prepared lid. Cook over boiling water for 1 hour. Turn out immediately onto a serving platter and top with the whipped cream and lightly toasted almonds.

Variation: Divide the beaten egg whites in half. Fold ½ cup prune purée into half the egg whites and ½ cup apricot purée into the other half. Put the apricot mixture into the pan, then place the prune mixture on top. Cook as directed above.

Grand Marnier Soufflé: Follow the above method, using 8 egg whites and ⅓ cup sugar instead and folding in 4 tablespoons Grand Marnier instead of the fruit purée. After cooking, dust with powdered sugar and serve with Soufflé Sauce.

"Double Boiler" Orange Soufflé

(4 servings)

4 egg whites
3 tablespoons sugar
3 tablespoons orange marmalade
1 cup heavy cream
2 tablespoons frozen orange juice concentrate, thawed
Zest of 1 orange, grated

Butter the top pan and lid of a 2½-quart double boiler and coat both with granulated sugar.

In a bowl beat the egg whites until foamy, add the sugar until stiff. With a wire whisk, gradually fold in the marmalade. Turn the mixture into the prepared double boiler and cover with the prepared lid. Cook over boiling water for 55 minutes.

In a bowl whip the cream and fold in the juice concentrate and orange zest. Turn the soufflé onto a serving plate and pour some of the sauce over it. Pass the remaining sauce separately.

"Double Boiler" Praline Soufflé

(8 servings)

    8 egg whites
    ¾ cup Praline Powder (*see below*)
    ⅓ cup Praline Powder
    Whipped cream flavored with vanilla

Follow the method for the Apricot or Prune Soufflé, combining the egg whites and the ¾ cup praline powder. After cooking, turn out and sprinkle the ⅓ cup praline powder over the top. Serve with whipped cream flavored with vanilla.

Praline Powder:

    1 cup sugar
    1 cup toasted almonds *or* pecans *or* hazelnuts

Butter a small baking sheet or plate. In a heavy saucepan or skillet melt the sugar until it is golden. Add the nuts and stir gently until they are well coated and light brown. Immediately turn out onto the buttered baking sheet. When the mixture has cooled, crack it into pieces. Place in a *dry* food processor or blender and process into a fine powder. Store in an airtight container.

Caramel Custard

(6 servings)

    ½ cup sugar
    2 tablespoons water
    2 cups milk
    4 tablespoons sugar
    1 teaspoon vanilla
    4 eggs, beaten

Preheat the oven to 325°.

To caramelize the mold: Mix the ½ cup sugar with the water in a 1-quart metal mold. Heat gently until the sugar dissolves; do not stir. Cook quickly over medium-high heat, lower the heat, and turn the mold carefully to coat it completely with the caramel (melted sugar). (Protect your hands with oven mitts or potholders.)

In a saucepan heat the milk with the 4 tablespoons sugar and the vanilla over medium-low heat (to avoid scalding). In a bowl beat the eggs and pour the hot milk mixture into them gradually, stirring constantly. Pour into the caramelized mold. Place the mold in a pan of hot water and bake for 30 to 40 minutes, until a knife inserted in the center comes out clean. Cool slightly and unmold onto a serving plate.

Chilled Apple Cream

(4–6 servings)

    1 cup sweetened applesauce
    ¼ teaspoon cinnamon
    ⅛ teaspoon nutmeg, or to taste
    1 teaspoon melted butter
    2 teaspoons lemon juice
    1 cup heavy cream, whipped

In a bowl combine the applesauce, cinnamon, and nutmeg with the butter and juice. Chill for 1 hour. Fold in the whipped cream and chill for 2 to 3 hours before serving.

Orange Blossom Bowl

(8 servings)

    12 double ladyfingers
    2 cups heavy cream
    2 tablespoons honey
    6 tablespoons frozen orange juice
       concentrate, thawed
    1 orange, peeled and sectioned,
       membranes removed (garnish)

Split the ladyfingers and line the bottom and sides of a 1½-quart glass dish. In a bowl beat the cream and honey until stiff. Fold in the orange concentrate. Spoon the mixture over the ladyfingers and chill for at least 4 hours. Garnish with the orange sections and serve.

Lemon Pudding

(8 servings)

    1 tablespoon unflavored gelatin
    ¾ cup cold water
    6 tablespoons lemon juice
    6 egg yolks
    1½ cups sugar
    Rind of 1 lemon, grated
    6 egg whites

In a small bowl soften the gelatin in cold water. In a saucepan warm the lemon juice over medium heat and dissolve the gelatin in it, stirring constantly. Beat the egg yolks with the sugar until light. Add the gelatin mixture and the lemon rind. Beat the egg whites until stiff and fold into the mixture. Pour into a 6-cup serving dish and refrigerate, preferably for 24 hours, before serving.

Lemon Bread Pudding

(4–6 servings)

  2 egg yolks
  ½ cup sugar
  2 cups milk
  1 cup day-old white bread cubes
  Grated rind of 1 lemon

Meringue:
  2 egg whites
  ¾ cup sugar
  Juice of 1 lemon

Preheat the oven to 325°. Butter a 6-cup casserole.

In a large bowl beat the egg yolks until light, adding the sugar gradually. Add the milk, bread cubes, and lemon rind. Pour into the buttered casserole. Bake for 45 to 60 minutes, until a knife inserted in the center comes out clean.

To make the meringue, beat the egg whites until soft peaks form, adding the sugar gradually. Add the lemon juice and reserve.

When the pudding is done, cover with the meringue and bake for an additional 30 to 35 minutes, until the meringue is slightly browned. Serve cool.

Frozen Rum Cream

(10 servings)

  4 egg yolks
  4 tablespoons sugar
  3 egg whites, stiffly beaten
  1½ cups heavy cream, whipped
  ½ cup rum

In a bowl beat the egg yolks and sugar until they are thick and light. Fold in the egg whites, the cream, and the rum. Freeze for at least 8 hours before serving.

The Russian Tea Room's Russian Cream

(6 servings)

  ½ cup water
  4 envelopes unflavored gelatin
  2 cups (1 pint) heavy cream
  ¼ cup sifted confectioners' sugar
  1 drop red food coloring
  1 quart vanilla ice cream, softened
  ⅓ cup slivered blanched almonds
  ⅓ cup grenadine syrup

Pour the water into a small bowl and sprinkle the gelatin over it. Stir to blend. Set the bowl in a pan of boiling water and dissolve the gelatin. While gelatin is dissolving, beat the cream until it is almost stiff. Beat in the sugar gradually, beating well after each addition; do not overbeat. Stir the food coloring into the whipped cream. Cool the gelatin to lukewarm. Place the softened ice cream in a large bowl. With a wire whisk, beat the cooled gelatin into the ice cream. Fold in the whipped cream. Spoon equal amounts of the cream into 6 individual dessert dishes or, preferably, stemmed wineglasses. Cover with plastic wrap and refrigerate for at least 4 hours. At serving time, sprinkle each dish with 1 tablespoon of the almonds and top with 1 tablespoon of the grenadine.

Note: Russian Cream has a lighter taste than ice cream and a marvelously airy consistency. Much loved at the Russian Tea Room in New York, it is a refreshing ending to a meal.

Summer Pudding

(6 servings)

7 thin slices white bread
Soft butter
3 cups blueberries
⅓ cup water
⅔ cup sugar (or to taste)
Heavy cream *or* sweetened whipped
    cream (optional)

Butter the bread lightly and line a 4-cup casserole with 6 of the slices, butter side out. In a saucepan cook the blueberries with the water and the sugar to taste for 10 minutes over medium heat. Pour the mixture into the bread-lined casserole. Place the remaining slice of bread, butter side up, on top and fold the edges of the other slices in to meet it. Place a saucer on top. Press down, and pour off the excess liquid. Reserve the liquid to use as a sauce. Chill for at least 6 hours, unmold, and serve. Pour some of the reserved sauce over each portion. Serve with heavy or whipped cream, if desired.

Variations: Raspberries or blackberries may be used instead of the blueberries.

Elizabeth Esterling's Rice Pudding

(6 servings)

½ cup converted long grain rice
½ teaspoon salt (optional)
1¾ cups boiling water
2 cups milk
2 large eggs
⅓ cup sugar
1½ teaspoons vanilla
½ cup raisins, softened 30 minutes in warm water, drained
Cinnamon
Cream (optional)

Preheat the oven to 350°.

In a saucepan add the rice and salt to the boiling water and simmer, covered, until the water is absorbed, 25 to 30 minutes. Add the milk and boil slowly until the mixture thickens slightly. Beat the eggs, sugar, and vanilla in a medium-size bowl and stir in the rice. Spoon the mixture into a buttered 6-cup casserole. Stir in the raisins. Sprinkle the top with cinnamon and place the casserole in a large baking pan. Add enough hot water to the pan to come halfway up the sides of the dish. Bake, uncovered, for 50 minutes to 1 hour, or until a knife inserted in the center comes out clean. Serve chilled or at room temperature, with cream if desired.

Quick Trifle

(6 servings)

1 8-inch cake layer, cut into pieces
3 tablespoons currant or raspberry jelly
3 tablespoons semi-dry sherry
1 package instant vanilla pudding mix
2½ cups milk
1 cup heavy cream, whipped

Cover the bottom of a 6-cup glass dish with the cake pieces. Spread on the jelly, then soak with the sherry. In a saucepan or mixing bowl, prepare the pudding with the 2½ cups milk. Pour the pudding over the cake. Chill. Top with the whipped cream and serve.

Zabaglione

(8 servings)

- 8 eggs, separated
- ½ cup confectioners' sugar
- ½ cup Marsala

In a bowl over hot water or in the top of a large double boiler, whip the egg yolks with the sugar over hot water until foamy; add the Marsala. Continue beating until fluffy and doubled in volume. Remove from the heat. Whip the egg whites until stiff and fold into the custard. Serve warm or cooled.

Note: Zabaglione is traditionally made in a copper pot with a rounded bottom and a long handle and beaten with a balloon whisk directly over the heat. But that takes a great deal of practice (and the pot is expensive and cannot be used for other dishes). The method above is far easier, and the result is quite delicious.

Creamy Zabaglione

(6 servings)

- ¼ cup sugar
- 1½ tablespoons unflavored gelatin
- ¾ cup Marsala
- 4 egg yolks
- 2 teaspoons vanilla
- 2 egg whites
- Pinch of cream of tartar
- 1 cup heavy cream
- 1 tablespoon sugar
- Sweetened whipped cream (optional)
- Candied violets (optional)

In a saucepan stir the sugar and gelatin into the Marsala and heat to dissolve. Beat the egg yolks over hot water in a double boiler until foamy; slowly add the gelatin mixture. Remove from the heat and add the vanilla. Whip the egg whites until foamy; add the cream of tartar. Beat until soft peaks form. Fold into the yolk mixture and cool. Whip the cream, gradually adding the sugar, and fold into the custard. Chill for several hours. Just before serving, decorate, if desired, with additional whipped cream and candied violets.

Extra-Rich Zabaglione

(4 servings)

    6   egg yolks
    1½   tablespoons sugar
    ⅓   cup light corn syrup
    5   tablespoons red wine

In the top of a double boiler combine all the ingredients. Cook over simmering water for about 3 to 4 minutes, beating until light. Serve warm or cooled.

Variations: Orange juice or dark rum can be substituted for the red wine.

Brown Betty

(8 servings)

    2   cups stale white bread cubes
    ½   pound butter, melted
    8   tart apples, pared, thinly sliced
    1   teaspoon cinnamon
    ½   cup brown sugar
    ½   cup water

Preheat the oven to 350°. Butter a 2-quart baking dish.

In a large bowl toss the bread cubes with the butter. Cover the bottom of the baking dish with half the apple slices. Mix the cinnamon with the sugar and sprinkle half of the mixture over the apples. Cover with half the bread cubes. Repeat with the second half of the ingredients. Sprinkle water over the top to keep it moist. Bake uncovered for 30 to 45 minutes. Serve with Hard Sauce.

Apple-Blueberry Crisp

(6–8 servings)

3 cups peeled sliced apples (should be tart)
2 cups fresh *or* dry-frozen blueberries
5 tablespoons brown sugar
2½ tablespoons flour
½ cup butter, melted
Heavy cream (optional)

Topping:
1 cup flour
¾ cup sugar
1 teaspoon baking powder
½ teaspoon salt
½ teaspoon cinnamon
1 egg

Preheat the oven to 350°.

Mix the apples and the berries and place in a buttered 6-cup casserole. Mix the brown sugar with the flour and sprinkle over the fruit. Sift the dry topping ingredients into a bowl. Add the egg and stir until the mixture is crumbly. Sprinkle the topping over the fruit and drizzle on the melted butter. Bake for 1 hour, until browned. Serve warm, with cream if desired.

Jean Anderson's Blackberry Cobbler with Whole-Wheat Shortbread Topping

(8 servings)

½ cup sugar
3 tablespoons cornstarch
2 teaspoons finely grated lemon rind
1 quart fresh blackberries, washed and stemmed
1 tablespoon unsalted butter, cut into bits

Topping:
1 cup sifted all-purpose flour
1 cup unsifted whole-wheat flour
⅓ cup sugar
1 tablespoon baking powder
¼ teaspoon salt
⅓ cup firmly packed vegetable shortening
5 tablespoons butter, cut into pats
½ cup milk

Combine the sugar, cornstarch, and the lemon rind in a large bowl, pressing out any lumps. Dump in the berries and toss well to mix. Set aside.

For the topping: Combine the two flours, the sugar, baking powder, and salt in a large bowl. Add the shortening and the butter and cut in, using a pastry blender, until uniformly crumbly. Drizzle in the milk, tossing briskly all the while with a fork just until the dough holds together.

Preheat the oven to 400°.

Stir the berry mixture well, and dump into an unbuttered 2-quart baking dish and dot evenly with the 1 tablespoon butter. Spoon the shortbread on top in clumps, then spread evenly until the berries are completely covered. Bake, uncovered, for 10 minutes; lower the heat to 350° and bake 25 to 30 minutes longer, or until the berries are bubbling and the shortbread is lightly browned. Cool for 30 minutes before serving.

Note: I like to drizzle a little light cream over each portion, but cobbler can certainly stand on its own merits.

Ice Creams, Sherbets & Ices

Blueberry Ice Cream
Cantaloupe Ice Cream
Frozen Chocolate Cream
Crunchy Lemon Ice Cream
Oreo Ice Cream
Chocolate-covered Peppermint Ice
   Cream
Raspberry Ice Cream
Easy Strawberry Ice Cream

Lemon Ice
Watermelon Ice
Grapefruit Ice
Orange Sherbet Parfait
Apple-Cranberry Sherbet
Elizabeth Schneider Colchie's Pine-
   apple Snow
Helen Witty's Sherbet with Apricot
   Sauce & Toasted Almonds

Blueberry Ice Cream

(2 quarts)

    2 pints blueberries
    1 cup sugar
    Pinch of salt
    2 cups heavy cream
    1 cup evaporated milk

In a saucepan mash the berries and cook with the sugar for 5 minutes over medium-low heat. Purée in a food mill; let cool. Add the salt, cream, and evaporated milk and stir to combine. Freeze in an ice cream maker or place in the freezer for 25 minutes. Remove from the freezer and stir to prevent the formation of ice crystals. Stir two more times at 25-minute intervals. Serve or store in the freezer.

Cantaloupe Ice Cream

(1 quart)

    2   cups cantaloupe
    1   cup sugar
    ⅔   cup water
    1½ cups heavy cream, whipped

In a blender or food processor chop the cantaloupe until smooth. In a small saucepan cook the sugar with the water for 5 minutes over medium-low heat. Add the syrup to the melon and mix well; let cool. Fold in the whipped cream. Freeze in an ice cream maker.

Frozen Chocolate Cream

(6–8 servings)

    ¼   cup sugar
    ½   cup water
    1   6-ounce package semisweet chocolate bits
    3   egg yolks
    1½ cups heavy cream

In a small saucepan combine the sugar and water and boil for 3 minutes. Place the chocolate bits in the pitcher of a blender, pour the hot syrup over them, and blend for 6 seconds. Add the egg yolks and blend for another 6 seconds or until smooth. Add the cream and blend for another 10 seconds. Pour into individual dishes, cover with foil, and freeze until firm, about 2 to 3 hours.

Crunchy Lemon Ice Cream

(1½ quarts)

    4 cups heavy cream
    2 cans frozen lemonade concentrate,
       thawed
    ½ cup sugar
    Pinch of salt
    4 tablespoons butter, melted
    ¼ cup corn flakes, crushed
    ¼ cup pecans, chopped
    ½ cup dark brown sugar

In a large bowl mix the cream, lemonade concentrate, sugar, and salt. Freeze in an ice cream mixer or in a freezer tray until partially firm. In a saucepan melt the butter, add the brown sugar, then mix in the corn flakes and pecans. When cool, swirl into the partially frozen ice cream, then freeze until firm.

Oreo Ice Cream

(6 servings)

    1 quart vanilla ice cream, softened
    2½ cups crumbled vanilla-cream-filled
       chocolate wafer cookies (Oreos)

In a large bowl combine the softened ice cream and the cookies. Pour the mixture into a serving dish, cover, and refreeze.

Chocolate-covered Peppermint Ice Cream

(2 quarts)

    1½ cups sugar
    ¼ cup water
    30 chocolate-covered peppermints
    6 egg whites
    1 tablespoon vanilla
    6 cups heavy cream, whipped

In a small saucepan, boil the sugar and water for 5 minutes; let cool. In the top of a double boiler melt the peppermints. In a large bowl beat the egg whites, adding the sugar syrup slowly. Add the vanilla, whipped cream, and the melted chocolate. Mix well. Freeze in a metal pan.

Raspberry Ice Cream

(1 quart)

⅔ cup sweetened condensed milk
1 tablespoon lemon juice
1 10-ounce package frozen raspberries, thawed and drained
1 cup heavy cream, whipped

In a bowl or blender combine the milk, lemon juice, and raspberries and blend until smooth. Fold the mixture into the whipped cream. Freeze in an ice cube tray for 2 to 3 hours.

Easy Strawberry Ice Cream

(4–6 servings)

1 10-ounce package sliced frozen strawberries
1 cup sugar
2 cups sour cream

In a bowl defrost the berries until they are soft but not completely thawed. Add the sugar and sour cream, stirring until well combined. Place in the freezer for 25 minutes. Remove from the freezer and stir to prevent the formation of ice crystals. Stir two more times at 25-minute intervals. Serve or store in the freezer.

Lemon Ice

(1½ quarts)

Rind of 2 lemons
2 cups plus 2 tablespoons sugar
3 cups water
2½ cups fresh lemon juice

In a food processor fitted with a steel blade chop the lemon rind with 1 cup of the sugar until fine. Combine with the remaining sugar and water in a saucepan and boil for 5 minutes. Add the lemon juice and the chopped rind and sugar and cool. Freeze.

Watermelon Ice

(2 quarts)

4 pounds watermelon, cut from rind, seeds removed
3 tablespoons lemon juice
2 tablespoons sugar
½ teaspoon salt

Cut the melon into 1-inch chunks. Purée in a food processor or blender with all the other ingredients. Freeze. To serve, process desired amount to soften it. Serve immediately.

Grapefruit Ice

(1 quart)

- 1½ cups water
- 1 cup sugar
- ½ cup lemon juice
- 2 cups grapefruit juice
- 1 egg white, lightly beaten

In a saucepan boil the water and sugar for 5 minutes. Cool, then add the fruit juices. Freeze in an ice cube tray. Place the frozen mixture in the bowl of a food processor and add the egg white. Process until creamy. Return to the freezer until firm.

Orange Sherbet Parfait

(4 servings)

- 1 pint orange sherbet
- 2 oranges, peeled and sectioned
- 4 sprigs of fresh mint (garnish)

Layer slightly softened sherbet and the orange sections in a parfait glass or wineglass, beginning and ending with the sherbet. Top with a slice of orange and a sprig of mint if desired. Freeze until ready to serve.

Variations: Use pineapple cubes instead of orange slices. Try raspberry sherbet with sliced peaches, or lemon sherbet with strawberry halves.

Apple-Cranberry Sherbet

(1½ quarts)

- 1 pound tart apples
- 1 pound cranberries
- 1 cup sugar
- ½ cup cranberry juice cocktail
- 2 tablespoons Calvados
- 2 egg whites

Pare, core, and coarsely chop the apples. In a food processor fitted with the steel blade, blend the apples, berries, and sugar for 30 seconds or until smooth. Strain if desired; add the juice and Calvados and process until frothy. Pour into a shallow pan and freeze until quite firm. Scrape into the processor and blend with the egg whites until fluffy. Refreeze. If crystals should form, process again before serving.

Elizabeth Schneider Colchie's Pineapple Snow

(6 servings)

1 small ripe pineapple, peeled, cored, and cut into chunks (about 3 cups)
2 tablespoons rum, any kind
6 tablespoons superfine sugar
2 egg whites
1 cup heavy cream, chilled
Small, ripe strawberries, hulled, washed, and halved (garnish)

In a food processor or by hand coarsely grate or shred the pineapple (there should be about 2 cups) and place in a bowl. Stir in the rum and 2 tablespoons of the sugar. Cover and refrigerate until ready to serve.

Beat the egg whites until fluffy in the small bowl of an electric mixer at medium speed. At high speed add the remaining sugar, 1 tablespoon at a time, beating for 1 minute after each addition. Whip the cream until it forms soft peaks. Using a rubber spatula, gently fold the whipped cream into the egg whites. Spoon the mixture into a sieve lined with a double layer of damp, fine-mesh cotton cheesecloth and set over a bowl. Cover and refrigerate for up to 5 hours.

To serve, loosen the cream carefully from the cheesecloth and put it into a large, chilled serving dish. With a rubber spatula, gently fold the pineapple mixture into the cream. Garnish with the strawberries and serve immediately.

Helen Witty's Sherbet with Apricot Sauce & Toasted Almonds

(4 servings)

1 jar apricot preserves
Dark Jamaican rum
1 ounce sliced blanched almonds
1 pint pineapple or lemon sherbet

In a bowl thin the apricot preserves with the rum to taste. Toast the almonds in a small skillet over medium heat, stirring until they are golden. Scoop the sherbet into serving dishes, spoon over the sauce, and top with the toasted almonds.

Note: Any remaining sauce can be stored in a jar in the refrigerator for later use.

Variation: Try preparing the sauce with brandy instead of rum.

Fruit Desserts

Fruit & Cheese with Wine
Brandied Fruit Compote
Honey Apples
Pennsylvania Dutch Apple Dessert
Apple Brandy Apples
Bananas Flambées
Cantaloupe Cocktail
Gooseberry Fool
Seedless Grapes in Brandy Cream
Oriental Oranges
Ambrosia
Peach Melba

Peaches in Chablis
Richard Sax's Italian Stuffed Peaches
Caramelized Pears
Barbetta Restaurant's Pears Baked in
    Red Wine
Poached Pears
Maurice Moore-Betty's Plums
    Grasmere
Tipsy Raspberries
Strawberries & Cream
Strawberries in Champagne
Strawberries Chantilly

Fruit & Cheese with Wine

Select several cheeses with authoritative flavors, such as Roquefort, Gorgonzola, Stilton, or Emmenthaler. For those who prefer a milder cheese, Monterey Jack, Edam, or Gouda may be added. A crock of cream cheese with walnuts is a nice addition, too.

Apples, pears, oranges, and grapes; berries, cherries, and strawberries — in season — are all appropriate. Arrange the fruits attractively in a bowl or basket and provide individual plates and fruit knives.

Accompany your dessert spread with a pleasing, full-bodied dry red wine.

Brandied Fruit Compote

(4 servings)

¾ cup seedless grapes
1 pear
1 apple
¼ cup apricot or plum brandy
1 tablespoon sugar
Whipped cream

Cut the grapes in half. Cut the pear in half; core, peel, and slice it. Peel, core, and slice the apple. In a large bowl combine the brandy and sugar. Add the fruit and toss. Cover with plastic wrap and refrigerate for 1 to 2 hours, stirring occasionally. Flavor the whipped cream with a little additional brandy. Divide the fruit into 4 individual compotes or serving dishes. Top each one with a dollop of the whipped cream.

Honey Apples

(6 servings)

6 tart apples, washed
½ cup honey
1½ teaspoons grated lemon rind
Ground nutmeg

Preheat the oven to 375°.

Core each apple, leaving the base intact. Place the apples in the bottom of a casserole that has a cover. Fill the apple cavities with the honey, add ¼ teaspoon of the lemon rind to each cavity, then sprinkle with the nutmeg. Cover the casserole and bake for 30 to 40 minutes. Remove the cover and bake for an additional 10 minutes or until apples are tender. Serve warm.

Pennsylvania Dutch Apple Dessert

(4–6 servings)

- 4 medium apples
- 1 cup brown sugar
- 2 tablespoons flour
- ½ teaspoon salt
- ½ teaspoon cinnamon
- ½ cup uncooked oatmeal
- ½ cup flour
- 6 tablespoons butter, melted

Preheat the oven to 350°. Butter the sides and bottom of an 8-inch-square baking pan.

Pare, core, and slice the apples. In a large bowl combine the brown sugar, 2 tablespoons flour, salt, and cinnamon. Add the apple slices and toss. Place the mixture in the prepared baking pan. Combine the oatmeal and the remaining flour. Sprinkle over the apples, then drizzle over the melted butter. Bake for 40–45 minutes. Serve warm.

Apple Brandy Apples

(6 servings)

- 6 baking apples (such as Cortland *or* Rome Beauty)
- ½ cup brown sugar
- ¾ teaspoon cinnamon
- 2 tablespoons butter, softened
- ½ cup water
- ½ cup Calvados *or* apple brandy
- 6 tablespoons mincemeat
- Heavy cream

Preheat the oven to 400°.

Core the apples, peel them one third of the way down, and place in a shallow baking dish. In a small bowl combine the brown sugar and cinnamon. Fill the apple cavities with this mixture and stuff 1 teaspoon of the soft butter into each apple. Combine the water and brandy and pour into the baking dish. Bake the apples for 30 minutes, basting frequently (the apples should be almost tender). Fill the apple cavities with the mincemeat and continue baking for 10 to 15 more minutes, basting two or three additional times. Serve warm; pass the cream separately.

Bananas Flambées

(4 servings)

    4 bananas, peeled
    Flour
    4 tablespoons butter
    6 tablespoons granulated sugar
    ¼ cup rum

Preheat the oven to 400°.

Roll the bananas in the flour to coat lightly, then sauté them briefly in the butter. Drain and place the bananas on an oven-proof serving platter. Sprinkle with 4 table-spoons of the sugar. Bake for 10 minutes or until the bananas puff up. Remove the platter from the oven and keep warm.

In a small saucepan over medium-low heat melt the remaining 2 tablespoons sugar with the rum. To serve, take the warm platter and the rum mixture to the table. Light the rum mixture, and pour, flaming, over the bananas.

Cantaloupe Cocktail

(8 servings)

    1 6-ounce can frozen lemon-lime drink
       concentrate, thawed
    4 cups cantaloupe balls
    8 sprigs mint

In a bowl or a bottle, combine the concentrate with 1 can of cold water and mix well. Chill for 1 hour. Divide the melon balls among 8 individual serving dishes. Pour over the lemon-lime mixture, garnish with the mint, and serve.

Gooseberry Fool

(4 servings)

    1½ cups canned gooseberries, drained
    ¾   cup heavy cream
    1   egg white, stiffly beaten
    Sugar to taste
    Blueberries or strawberries (garnish)

In a food processor or blender purée the gooseberries. Whip the cream in a large bowl. Fold the gooseberry purée and the beaten egg white into the cream. Sweeten the mixture if

(Preceding Pages) Fruit & Cheese with Wine

necessary. Divide among 4 individual serving dishes; garnish with the blueberries or strawberries.

Note: This mixture can also be spooned into prebaked tartlet shells and garnished as above.

Seedless Grapes in Brandy Cream

(6 servings)

- 2 pounds seedless white grapes, washed and stemmed
- ¼ cup brandy
- ½ cup heavy cream
- ½ cup sour cream
- 2 tablespoons confectioners' sugar, sifted
- 4 tablespoons dark brown sugar (or ½ cup, depending on the grapes' sweetness)

Place the grapes in a serving dish and sprinkle with the brandy, turning them with a spoon to coat them evenly. Whip the cream, adding the sour cream and confectioners' sugar. Pour the cream mixture over the grapes and sprinkle over the brown sugar. Freeze for about 10 minutes or chill in the refrigerator for at least 1 hour.

Oriental Oranges

(10 servings)

- 3 cups water
- 3 cups sugar
- 8 navel oranges, peeled
  Zest from 6 oranges, julienne
- ¼ cup orange liqueur

Make a syrup of the water and the sugar, boiling it to the "soft ball" stage (235° on a candy thermometer, or when a spoonful of syrup forms a soft ball when dropped into cold water). Cook the orange peel strips in the syrup for a few minutes, until translucent. Remove the peel from the syrup and drain. Reserve the syrup and candied peel.

Slice the oranges and place in a glass or silver serving bowl. Add the liqueur to the reserved syrup and pour over the oranges. Place the candied strips on top of the oranges and chill for at least 1 hour before serving.

Ambrosia

(6 servings)

- 3 cups sliced oranges, with juice
- ¾ cup shredded coconut, fresh if possible
- ½ cup blanched almond pieces

In a bowl sprinkle the orange slices and juice with the coconut and almonds and chill well.

Variation: Sliced bananas may be added at the last minute. Classic ambrosia, however, is prepared as above.

Peach Melba

(6 servings)

- 2 10-ounce packages frozen raspberries, thawed and drained (reserve juice)
- ½ cup sugar
- 1 15-ounce can peaches, drained and chilled *or* 6 ripe peaches

Fresh mint leaves (garnish)

Push the raspberries through a sieve or use a food mill to remove the seeds. In a bowl combine the berries with the sugar. Add the reserved raspberry juice to achieve the desired consistency. Chill. Pour the raspberry sauce over the peaches in individual compotes and garnish with mint leaves.

Peaches in Chablis

(4 servings)

- ½ pound sugar
- 1 cup water

Juice of 1 orange
Strip of lemon peel
Strip of orange peel

- 1 cinnamon stick, broken up
- 2½ pounds small ripe peaches, washed
- 1 cup Chablis

Whipped cream

In a large saucepan combine the sugar, water, and orange juice. Add the citrus peels, cinnamon pieces, and peaches. Cook, covered, over medium-high heat for 15 minutes. Add the wine and cook, uncovered, for 15 minutes, or until the peaches are tender. Allow to cool. Remove the peaches from the liquid, peel, and place in a deep serving dish. Cook the reserved liquid over medium heat for 5 minutes, making a light syrup. Pour the syrup over the peaches and chill. Serve very cold. Top each serving with whipped cream.

Strawberries in Champagne

Richard Sax's Italian Stuffed Peaches

(6 servings)

- 6 large, ripe peaches
- ½ cup (approximately) raspberry preserves
- 12 Italian macaroons (*amaretti*), coarsely crumbled
- 4 tablespoons unsalted butter (½ stick), cut into bits
- ½ cup Amaretto (or more)

Preheat the oven to 350°.

Cut the peaches in half, remove and discard the stones, and scoop out a small amount of the pulp from the center of each half. Chop this pulp coarsely and reserve it. Arrange the peach halves in a baking dish.

Smear a spoonful of raspberry preserves into each peach cavity, then place a bit of the reserved pulp on top. Spoon a share of the macaroon crumbs into each cavity, then dot with the butter.

Sprinkle a little of the Amaretto on each peach half. Pour water into the pan to a depth of about ⅛ inch to prevent sticking. Bake until tender, about 20 minutes, basting occasionally with more Amaretto if desired. Serve warm or at room temperature.

Note: Peaches prepared in this manner are remarkable both for their glamorous perfume and sophisticated simplicity.

Caramelized Pears

(8 servings)

- 8 firm Bartlett pears
- 4 ounces butter
- Juice of ½ lemon
- Grated nutmeg
- Ground cinnamon
- 1 cup brown sugar
- ½ cup bourbon, warmed
- 1½ cups crème fraîche *or* whipped cream

Peel the pears, cut in half, and remove the cores. To prevent darkening, drop the pears into a bowl of water containing the lemon juice. Melt the butter over low heat in a fairly large skillet that has a cover and sauté the pears, cut side down first, until brown. Turn. When browned on both sides, dust generously with the nutmeg and cinnamon. Sprinkle with the brown sugar and let cook over low heat, covered, for 15 minutes to caramelize. Flame the bourbon and pour over the pears. Keep the pears warm, covered, until ready to serve. Pass the crème fraîche or whipped cream separately.

Barbetta Restaurant's Pears Baked in Red Wine

(6 servings)

- 1 cup Burgundy (or more as needed)
- ½ cup sugar
- 10 whole cloves
- 6 brown winter pears or other firm pears, whole, with stems intact, washed and dried
- Heavy cream (optional)

Preheat the oven to 450°.

Place the wine, sugar, and cloves in a baking dish and stir together. Add the pears, stems up. Place in the oven, stirring the juices to dissolve the sugar. Spoon the syrup over the pears.

Bake the pears until tender, spooning the juices over them every 5 minutes or so. They should be done in 45 minutes to 1 hour, depending on the size and variety. If at any time the liquid begins to cook away too much, add more wine. When the pears are tender, turn off the oven, baste them again, and let them sit for another 10 minutes. Remove from the oven, remove the cloves from the syrup, baste the pears again, and cool. Serve with their syrup and cool cream, if desired.

Note: This simple dessert brings to mind the lovely glazed, crinkled pears seen in *trattorias* throughout Italy.

Poached Pears

(6 servings)

- 6 ripe pears
- 4 cups good sauterne
- ¼ cup sugar (or more to taste)
- Juice of 1 lime

Peel the pears, cut them in half, and remove the cores. In a saucepan bring the sauterne just to a boil and poach the pears in the simmering wine until tender, about 20 minutes, adding the sugar as necessary. Cool the pears in the liquid until they reach room temperature, taking care that they are completely covered by the wine. Stir in the lime juice and refrigerate until ready to serve.

Maurice Moore-Betty's Plums Grasmere

(6–8 servings)

2½–3 pounds red plums, rinsed, halved, and pitted
2 tablespoons sugar
1 cup flour
Pinch of baking soda
1 tablespoon ground ginger
1 stick unsalted butter, softened, cut into small pieces
⅓ cup (packed) light brown sugar
⅓ cup granulated sugar
1 cup heavy cream, lightly whipped (garnish)
Crème fraîche *or* sour cream (optional)

Preheat the oven to 350°.

In an 8- by 11- by 1½-inch ovenproof dish, arrange the plums, cut side up. Sprinkle the sugar over the plums.

Sift together into a mixing bowl the flour, soda, and ginger. With your fingertips, work in the butter until the mixture resembles coarse cornmeal. Add the brown and granulated sugars and mix thoroughly. Spread the topping evenly over the fruit.

Bake for 30 minutes or until the top is golden, but not brown. Serve warm, passing separately the lightly whipped cream. If you wish, fold into the cream a little crème fraîche or sour cream.

Note: If you want to glaze the top, just before serving place the plums under a preheated broiler until the topping is bubbly and caramelized.

Tipsy Raspberries

(8 servings)

1 quart raspberries
1 bottle red Burgundy
½ cup sugar

Place the raspberries in a glass bowl. In a small saucepan heat ¼ cup of the wine and dissolve the sugar in it. Cool and pour over the berries. Add enough additional red wine to cover. Mix gently and chill before serving.

Strawberries & Cream

(4–6 servings)

2 pints strawberries, washed, hulled, and sliced
⅔ cup sour cream
⅓ cup light brown sugar
Brown sugar (topping)
Sour cream (topping)

In a bowl gently combine the strawberries, sour cream, and brown sugar. Divide mixture among individual serving dishes and top each with 1 tablespoon sour cream and 1 teaspoon brown sugar.

Strawberries in Champagne

(8 servings)

- 1 quart strawberries, hulled
- ½ cup sugar
- 1 bottle dry champagne, chilled

In a large bowl mix the strawberries gently with the sugar. Refrigerate. Just before serving, place the strawberries in champagne glasses or a glass serving bowl. Cover the berries with the champagne and serve.

Peaches in Champagne: Substitute 8 peaches, peeled, for the strawberries and add 1 tablespoon lemon juice to the peaches and sugar.

Strawberries Chantilly

(8 servings)

- 2 cups strawberries, washed, hulled, and coarsely chopped
- ¼ cup sugar
- 3 meringue shells, purchased or home-made
- 2 cups heavy cream, whipped

Place the berries in a bowl and sprinkle with the sugar. Chill for at least 2 hours. Crumble the meringues. Fold the strawberries and meringues into the whipped cream and serve immediately.

Sauces

Amaretto Cream Sauce
No-Cook Fudge Sauce
Sauce Cardinal
Hard Sauce
Sauce Sabayon
Sauce for Soufflés or Fruit Desserts
Hot Strawberry Sauce

Amaretto Cream Sauce

(1 cup)

1 cup sour cream
1½ tablespoons Amaretto
3 tablespoons confectioners' sugar, sifted
1 teaspoon almond extract

In a bowl combine all the ingredients and blend thoroughly. Cover and chill. Serve over fresh fruit. Blueberries, strawberries, pineapple, and bananas are an excellent combination.

Sauce Cardinal

(About 5 cups)

1 10-ounce package frozen raspberries, thawed
½ cup sugar
1 tablespoon lemon juice
Kirsch to taste
4 cups strawberries, hulled and sliced

Purée the raspberries in a blender or food processor. Strain. Add the sugar, juice, and kirsch and mix until the sugar has dissolved. Add the strawberries and chill. Serve over ice cream and fruit.

No-Cook Fudge Sauce

(1½ cups)

¾ cup hot milk or hot coffee
1 cup sugar
2 teaspoons vanilla
4 ounces unsweetened chocolate, cut up

Put the ingredients in a blender in the order listed. Blend on high speed until the chocolate has liquefied. Serve immediately over ice cream, cake, or in milkshakes.

Hard Sauce

(2 cups)

1 cup confectioners' sugar
½ cup butter
1 egg white, beaten stiff
¼ cup dark rum

In a mixing bowl or food processor cream the sugar and butter. Fold in the egg white and rum. Freeze until hard. Serve with Brown Betty.

Sauce Sabayon

(1½ cups)

- ½ cup sugar syrup (3 tablespoons sugar to 1 tablespoon water, cooked for 5 minutes over medium heat)
- 4 egg yolks

Beat the syrup and egg yolks in the top of a double boiler or over hot water until creamy. Cool. Serve with the Frozen Avocado Soufflé.

Sauce for Soufflés or Fruit Desserts

(6 servings)

- 2 egg yolks
- 1 cup confectioners' sugar
- 1 cup heavy cream, whipped
- 2 tablespoons liqueur (brandy, Cointreau, Amaretto, Tia Maria)

In a bowl beat the egg yolks and gradually add the sugar. Chill. Just before serving, combine the egg mixture with the whipped cream and flavor with a liqueur.

Hot Strawberry Sauce

(2 cups)

- 1 pint strawberries, washed, hulled, and halved *or*
- 1 package frozen strawberries, thawed
- Sugar to taste (¼ cup for fresh berries)
- 1½ tablespoons Grand Marnier

In a saucepan combine the berries and sugar and simmer over low heat until just soft. Remove from the heat, stir in the Grand Marnier, and serve immediately. This is a wonderful complement to the Frozen Amaretto Soufflé.

Index

Make your home special

Since 1922, millions of men and women have turned to *Better Homes and Gardens* magazine for help in making their homes more enjoyable places to be. You, too, can trust *Better Homes and Gardens* to provide you with the best in ideas, inspiration and information for better family living.

In every issue you'll find ideas on food and recipes, decorating and furnishings, crafts and hobbies, remodeling and building, gardening and outdoor living plus family money management, health, education, pets, car maintenance and more.

For information on how you can have *Better Homes and Gardens* delivered to your door, write to: Mr. Robert Austin, P.O. Box 4536, Des Moines, IA 50336.